PURE CARING

The path to the one heart through healing, caregiving and everyday experience

By

Janie Piano

Zen Way Press

Seattle, Washington

Copyright © 2009 by Janie Piano

All rights reserved. No part of this book may be reproduced or utilized in any form or by any means, electronic or mechanical, including photocopying, recording, or by any information storage and retrieval system, without permission in writing from the publisher or author.

ISBN: 978-0-578-03171-2

Cover photo by Alyssa Evans

Cover design by Bruce D. Fleming

Dedication

This book is dedicated to the inherent wisdom of the universe that provides what is needed at just the right time for spiritual growth... all the offerings being stepping stones leading to the Master, that shines the light of truth, revealing the stillness, beauty and glory that lies within one's own being. With great love and gratitude thank you to my Guru, Swami-G, for blessing this one with God vision. Thank you for setting so many on the path to this beauty, and pranams to the dear sages under her care that now offer this light to humanity.

This book is also dedicated to those who are now on the spiritual path — may one keep moving forward into greater depths and eventually come to know our true nature. The writing is also dedicated to those who are timid or uncertain about how to begin... it matters not who you are or where you come from — please start!!! Begin to take steps as realization is within you and not separate — not out there somewhere. Realization is the most ordinary, natural state of being and can be discovered within ordinary circumstances. Blessings and pranams to those that begin and continue forward — one is bound to come to know this truth. Keep going dear ones!!!

I would also like to thank Julia Hale, Claire Mooney, Thea Graham, Amy Hard and Mary Falkenstein for their time editing the manuscript. Sachi Ananda for editing, technical support and publishing. Thank you to Tony Simpson for doing the glossary. With much gratitude, thank you for this wonderful seva. Thank you to Ken Hiraiwa for the initial graphic design work. Thank you to Bruce D. Fleming for the cover design. Thank you to my son, Judah Piano, for his help on the technical pieces. Also, thank you to those that read through the writing and offered support.

Janie Piano — Swami Siddhananda

This book is about life and bringing spirituality into everyday experience. Hospice and caregiving are used as a means to express this message.

May the reader not focus on the hospice/caregiving aspect so much that the true message gets lost, as the teachings contained in this book direct one towards the universal soul and are in no way limited to a particular role or circumstance.

The writing, if you allow it, will meet you where you are now, in this moment, as you are, no matter what background, position or place. We are all of one essence and not one is shielded from the trials and tribulations of existence — the human experience.

Contents

Introduction   *1*
Foreword   *7*

Part I: Pure Caring

1. The Experience of Pure Caring   23
2. The Body/Mind   77
3. Emotions   89

Part II: The Path to the One Heart

4. Healing Touch   115
5. Tools and Practices   177
6. Meditation Exercises from Swami-G   197
7. Spiritual Teachers and Masters   207

Endnote   *221*
Glossary   *245*

Rise up
sweet one and sing
glory is the seed that waits
to be watered by your joy
come to the river where there are no gates
step in and feel the cool against
your skin
after such a long, long walk

Taste of the fruit that sits heavy on the vine
sweet heaven
right at hand
breathe in the fragrance of truth that
is as free as air and as lovely
as the smell of spring blooming
rise up sweet one and sing
God's beauty is all around
everywhere and always

Beautiful child
you are a spark of thy love
and thy life
like a river that runs down
mountainside
flowing into the great waterfall
and rejoicing in the ocean nature
this is your soul
oh dear one move easily this way
towards truth

Walk this way
through the open spaces
curving and weaving your way around that which is
not giving
winding your way like the river
over the boulders and stones
parting easily around that which is solid
dear one flow like this towards truth

Open this way
like a small child that has been without mother
for a long, long time
and sees her bright face appear on
a sunny spring morning
and runs open-armed smiling in full rejoicement
oh heart friend open this way to the truth

Play this way
like an orchestra with every sound
in tune with the other
not one missed beat, resounding as one
flowing, flowing and dissolving in space
play this way my friend
in harmony with grace

Be this way
within your true nature
like the simple tree on the hillside
like the simple stone by the gate with
the dandelion, the lilac and bright buds

on the branches
like the bird in flight
and the squirrel that plays
like the child that giggles
be this way so simple
within your true nature
as this is where truth lies

Oh child of the spirit
within, there is a wellspring
that rises up to quench the thirst
a wealth of nutrients
that makes that which is crooked, straight
that which is stagnant, fluid
that which holds, open
that which is hidden, brilliant
that which has wandered, still
that which calls, silent
that which is separate, whole

O friend, be this way
within your true nature
so simple
this is the song of your heart
and it is singing now
Om

Introduction

When internal boundaries dissolve, washing clean all separative views such as, "I am this" and "you are that," pure caring manifests as the divine healing force of the universe, which is unconditionally all loving and protecting. As we begin to dedicate our lives to seeking true healing through spirit, and the mind begins to quiet down, settling into the heart, love and caring are experienced in a fuller manner — more universal, not confined to a particular role or personality, but much freer and abiding. Love is experienced as flowing from the fountain of pure, inherent intelligence within — the God essence that is the jewel, the nourishment and heart of all of life. The spiritual practices in this writing help one to become attuned to this divine flow and from there, all action, speech and manner are moved by grace and can be nothing but careful, caring and compassionate, which is the movement and force of God's love. This is pure caring.

The inspiration for this book

Recently, I attended a hospice conference in the Pacific Northwest. The practical information was very good and the stories very touching (as all hospice stories are), but it was the discussions on "soul work" that left one unsatisfied. There is no doubt the messages delivered by the speakers at the conference came from well-intentioned, very experienced hospice staff who do beautiful work in the community. This cannot be denied, but what was noticed in the lectures was that the majority of the discussion centered around personal pain, as well as a sense of doership or ego involvement in caregiving. It is this screen of personhood with its history of pain and ego investment in our work that separates us from the healing forces inherent in the universe and in turn perpetuates internal isolation, leading to burnout and fueling the urge to pull away into a shell of protection.

The feel of the information given at the conference was like traditional therapy — quite stale and artificial, solidifying roles such as the "suffering one in need" and the "helper who has all the answers." I would imagine that I am not the only one who felt this way. I know the staff I work with in Seattle have a very rich spiritual background and are quite mature, having passed through a variety of caregiving and life experiences and are probably thirsty for more substance for the soul than what was offered at the conference. There was simply no talk of unity, though there was some brief discussion on getting ourselves out of the way when working, nothing that could truly be of use on a daily basis was given. It was a disappointment to see work that is so extremely rich for spiritual awakening not discussed to its full potential.

Pure Caring is a flowering of seeing the need for a new light to be shed on the healer/caregiver role. This book is not limited to this subject, however, and can be of use to anyone who is interested in embarking on a spiritual path or who is simply ready to look at everyday experience in a different light. What is offered in this writing is a foundation for spiritual practices that aid in bringing balance to the mind and heart. It is really dependent on how deep one is willing to go, as the universe will offer the aid needed every step of the way when the heart is sincere. It is hoped that this book illumines the inherent help and support that is everlastingly present in the universe.

May this book honor and enhance the loving, selfless work of caregiving that has been witnessed time and time again in the community — in nursing homes, adult family homes, private homes, by nurses, social workers, comfort therapists, alternative therapists, occupational therapists, home health aides, counselors, volunteers, doctors, family members, chaplains, neighbors and friends, as well as all those who work behind the scenes making phone calls, doing paperwork, supervising, managing and whatever it takes to help prepare the way for the one in need to receive care. May this book honor all who join in to help relieve the suffering of others. It is hoped that *Pure Caring* will help to lift the burden and bring fresh life to the heart and a lighter step to the walk when doing this beautiful work. It has been an honor to witness and be a part of the beautiful experience of caregiving.

Personal Story

The heart has been stirred to know God since childhood. I did not begin routine spiritual practices however until after my son was born in my early thirties. A strong urge came over me to meditate and I went about doing so in an extremely disciplined manner, meditating for hours with my eyes covered with a cloth so as to not be distracted by externals, sitting in graveyards contemplating the decay of the form, allowing whatever bubbled from the unconscious to surface, spending many entire days being mindful and then meditating some more. Daily, I would pray to be made useful, to know God and be of assistance to humanity. This is how several years passed. Although I had experienced spiritual phenomena from a young age, I was totally unprepared for the mystical world that opened up as a result of these intense spiritual practices, which left me ungrounded and shaken. Up until this point I had gone about the business of seeking truth totally on my own, not understanding the full picture, not understanding that a spiritual master was the missing link to help guide the sincere seeker to completion. It was not until after I met my Guru, Swami-G, four to five years later that I understood that these strange experiences taking place were classic symptoms of a Kundalini awakening. I was not seeking a Guru or seeking to awaken Kundalini, as I had no clue of the significance of either; I just truly desired to be free of the round of suffering so as to be of service to others.

One day, when Kundalini symptoms had spun out of control leaving fear, illness, depression and shaking, I went to the computer and typed in "Kundalini." Swami-G's name (then known as Ganga Karmokar) popped up on the screen. I don't recall any other writing except that she wrote that the Kundalini journey had completed for her and she was willing to help others through the experience. I wrote to her, not knowing what would take place from there. The very next day, I received answers to my questions that stopped the mind as I read. The responses were very clear, very helpful and calming. It was obvious that the one responding was a mystic and spoke from direct experience — which is what the heart was craving.

Swami-G was in India at the time of our first correspondence. She asked me in one of the first mails where I lived. She said she wanted to know because she was coming to visit Capitol Hill in Seattle (where her daughter lived) and wondered if I lived anywhere close. I told her that this is *exactly* where I lived! So much has changed since meeting my dear Guru. The world has taken on a very different look. Colors are deeper. Sounds are rich with vibration — moving, dancing, swaying, a beautiful dance! The mind stills daily, revealing an emptiness that feels as if immersed in the clearest, deepest pool — such depth of beauty, such stillness. Kundalini (Shakti) is still in motion, but most of the time, there is a witnessing and there is love that flows from the true heart of all, the one essence. There is a flow that arises from pure beingness. This is not to say that the inward journey is without challenge. It is extremely difficult, but worth every minute of toil as one moves from being caught in mundane consciousness with the dullness of just existing, to pure life, always fresh — in the full play and hands of God.

Since meeting Swami-G, I have taken Sannyas (the vows of a Hindu monk). The Sannyas name given by my Guru is Sage Swami Siddhananda-Puri.

Love and Om.

... And now, for those who are interested, may we go deeper...

Foreword

One must begin somewhere...

Any goal worth accomplishing takes preparation, effort and sacrifice. It can be seen throughout history, the great characters that personified these hearty qualities have accomplished magnificent feats — achievements that take the breath away and leave one wondering — "How did they manage to do that?" "Where did the drive come from?" These fine, awe inspiring personages of present and past literally drink, eat and live the goal — they do not settle for the less substantial food of hope, wishing and empty talk... the obstacles that come into the path in no way hindering, but lending potent fuel to the heart and mind to help surge them onward. The sincere seeker of God is of this same stalk, the very strong discriminative powers working endlessly, sifting out the perishable food of the transient that offers nothing, but sorrow, disease and death and imbibing in the sweet ambrosia nectar of God essence that brings internal strength and fortitude even through the rockiest part of the journey.

What brings endurance to spiritual challenge? This is a very important question because without stamina, there is little reserve to walk the path. Strength is depleted all too quickly and one finds themselves right back where they began, possibly in more despair — giving up or justifying — solidifying the same position that at one point the heart so desperately cried to be free of. The desire to be free of all that binds, and the willingness to face and continue forward through all obstacles that manifest needs to come to the surface and saturate the being with its incessant celestial hum, drowning out the call of lower desires and putting them in their proper place. The longing to be free is a very common desire — it is the willingness to endure that is the rarity. It is this union of pure desire and willingness that sifts out the student that has the chance to make it to the summit and enter union with the divine.

If one is interested in beginning the ascent to the summit, it takes preparation — it takes dedicated training. And for the ones unprepared, the ones that have put no time into practice, these ones often show up with an expectant, demanding attitude, leaving no room for the light of truth to enter... no ears to hear God's directions. Due to this lack of preparation, oftentimes there is a fall, which we call a spiritual casualty. This is why, if one is serious about beginning — it is urged to start to become fit within. This has nothing to do with strengthening the ego... instead this process is one of releasing and letting go so that innate knowing[1] can be uncovered and one is able to hear the guidance of the universal heart. This book offers spiritual direction that helps uncover pure desire that will bring drive and endurance to practice and give one a chance at the birthright of internal freedom.

Selflessness

There is an innate selflessness and sacrifice within us all. We can easily see this through the protection a mother and father give to the child... there is no thought involved in this process... it is a spontaneous flow of unconditional love. But there is a shadow that falls on this innate way of being as we move about our daily activities — it is the shadow of *me and mine* that stifles the full expression of our natural understanding: that we are not individual entities working only for ourselves, but indeed we belong and come from a much richer existence that is of one essence — that is not concerned about individual loss, but ready, willing and able to do whatever good is needed for the whole.

The Sage

As always, there is a paradox in the wisdom of the universe of which the man of God is no exception. Though the sage has gained this grace through extraordinary, Herculean type efforts, the heart, mind and personal will need to become as soft,

---

[1] A good name for innate knowing is God's directions.

flexible, sensitive, gentle, giving and open than anything ever imagined to receive the majesty that this one embodies. And where did this great one that now stands as illumined as the sun, that has brought waves of beings towards the radiant pure light of the divine and by his mere presence, altered the consciousness and brought so many to a higher level — where did this one begin? With one step. Though it was lifetimes ago, it started with *one step* (for one has to start somewhere), but this one kept going... and did not stop and the result of this effort is in the product: the sage that has walked this earth from beginningless time, bringing humanity back to reality, back to the truth. A gift beyond measure.

Anyone can begin a spiritual path. It does not matter who you are or what your history is because God's mercy resides ever-present in the open moment. It is this grace that offers endless opportunities and a continuous flow of forgiveness.

May the dear readers whose interest is still sparked find something of what is needed in the teachings that help bring strength and further clarity to their search.

Many Paths, One End

Although Hindu terminology is used in this writing, expression from any religious tradition would suffice as all religious paths meet and enter the same heart. When someone tells me that I am Hindu, I reply that I am not — this does not ring true for me. There is no loyalty to any particular religion;

rather there is an openness to all religions and an understanding that humanity is of one heart. How can there be a path that excludes another from myself? We are one.

Religious practices are meant to support one internally all the while tearing away the outer coverings that hide the center or source. Unfortunately much of religion has been personalized and clouded by dogma. The treasure of the ancient teachings that intended to bring unity and harmony has been misinterpreted. Many have pushed these teachings away due to past conditionings and also not taking the time to look deeper. It is a shame. When I met Swami-G, it was a pleasure to experience the infusion of life and love brought to Christianity, Buddhism, Zen, Hinduism — each and every religion containing the same weaving, yet with a little different expression, a little different twist — all treasures of truth. Many paths, one end. I ask that you see all religions in this writing. Look through the printed words to feel the human experience and beyond this, the oneness of all of life. There is no separation. All want to be loved. All want to be free of suffering. All want to be at peace (even though some appear to have strayed so very far away); still the desire is to be whole.

Whatever religious practices the heart is drawn to, it is optimal to remain there and deepen devotion, grace and love through that path. As a garden's beauty is enhanced by the variety of many flowers of varying shades and hues, so is the universal soul beautified by the expression of pure love through diversity. To honor one path with complete surrender and devotion is to honor all paths that lead this way.

Hinduism

It has been a great blessing to be exposed to Hinduism as the symbolism is extremely rich and so clearly expresses the path of yoga (union with the divine), which is the culmination of all religious paths.

Hinduism, also known as "Sanatana Dharma" or "the everlasting religion," is not a religion in the traditional sense; it is more a way of life. Hinduism does not have a starting point in history. There is no personality at the center as founder (the universe is the center) and it has no church. Hinduism has a profusion of gods and goddesses that are worshipped as manifestations of the supreme God — Brahman (the unchanging, infinite, transcendent reality). Hindu deities are rich with symbolism and serve as representations of the internal journey.

The Shiva lingum symbolizes the seed state or the essence of the entire cosmos, which is pure consciousness, pure awareness without content, the stillness in movement, the silence in sound. The lingum is the unmanifest.

The active power or manifest energy of Brahman is Shakti, which means power, force, energy. Anything that can be seen, heard or felt; anything that moves — this is Shakti. She is the feminine aspect of creation, also known as the divine mother. Shiva is the male aspect, Shakti, his expression. Like the silent deep, rich dark earth is Shiva — Shakti, the bright flower of manifestation that rises from this depth. The two are one, in union — the core or center of being (Shiva) is what brings life to Shakti (the play of the universe).

The unmanifest seed state, pure consciousness or God consciousness is the aim of spiritual practice. Shakti is the energy that does the work to get one there by removing the illusive coverings of mind that have built up over time from ignorance. Ignorance is attachment to body and mind (ego), which casts a shadow over the heart and shields one from seeing the true essence.

The Path

Spiritual work or sadhana is called "The Path" because there is some distance to go before one enters what has been termed "nirvana," "bliss," "no-mind" or "enlightenment." This is the path of surrender or letting go. It is not the path of accumulating, of creating a bigger and grander self-image. It is the path of allowing, of waiting and watching, of trust. It is heart centered, not control centered. It is universe centered, not *me and mine* centered. It takes dedication and very hard work to break down the tough shell of ego — in a word — *time*. In time all things change. They may not change when we want them to or how we want them to, but they do change.

Only we alone can place our feet on the path, however shaky we feel. We must walk it for ourselves and we walk it because we think well enough of ourselves to strive to be the best we can be, to reclaim our true nature which is our natural birthright. On this path we must be willing to face our fears, to die to our long held belief patterns that we are such and such, that we are this much or this little, that life is a certain way, that the future will be this way. We face our fear of uncertainty. We doubt that which we took to be certain. On this path we watch the body. We question who we are. *Are we this body? Is this all we are?* We soften into life, go with the flow of the current instead of struggling upstream, exhausting ourselves trying to have it our way. We let life have its way and just be. Slowly, a connection to something greater is revealed; for without spirituality there is no common thread that links us. We continually run ahead of our self, chasing desire after desire, running from our fears. On this path we allow the shadows we feel are chasing us to be revealed as just that — shadows with no substance — a thing with no power in itself and the mist begins to clear. Union with the divine source, the source from which all life springs, is the ultimate achievement of a lifetime; all else falls away, dies away, continuing the cycle of birth, decay, death and rebirth.

Sincere spiritual practice is heart centered. We begin with the heart, soften into life, melt down and rest in it. We may then begin to listen with innocence, without judgment and expectation. Spiritual work helps to soften blocks built up that shut out what we refuse to see. It is our refusal to see that keeps a part of us dead, and gives rise to tendencies towards addiction, depression and fear. But if we let up on ourselves, allow the fullness of ourselves room to breathe, things begin to turn around over time, and the constriction lets up. Breathing easier one step at a time, the consciousness begins to shift. There is an insight never before revealed, something so new to the mind that it shakes it up, leaving one hungry for more and we continue to walk through the highs and the lows of it. This is the path of cleansing and the pearl of great price is enlightenment. Yet nothing is really lost; only the suffering persona you thought you once were vanishes like a nightmare once dreamt long ago in childhood, a misty wisp of nothing, never to return.

All progress made is never lost.

The lotus blooms in the mud

a silent witness to all creation

the stars incandescent

emit the rays of the astral sun

no words, just pure energy, warmth and light

so my lips are still,

in the presence of my Guru...

Joy intoxicated, peace intoxicated, healing intoxicated

I bow to the radiance which flowers through Guru...

—*Lavani*

Guru

"Guru's words are the words of the seed of your being, the Truth of your heart which is one heart." —Swami-G

Over time, through dedicated sadhana, the blaze of love that burns reveals a consuming desire to know God. When the layer that separates one from the universal heart or supreme self has been thinned enough through the hard work of suffering, longing, wondering, questioning, loving, hoping and prayer, the Guru manifests. The Guru means "weighty one" or "one of great importance." Guru is the dispeller of all shadow. It is the Guru that, through initiation, helps transform the seeker's path from the ordinary path to the path of truth.

The Guru has different methods of transmitting the power of pure consciousness, but mostly mantras, transmission of energy and meditation practices are given. These practices hold an extremely high charge as they are transmitted from one who rests in pure consciousness and aid in breaking up the cyclic pattern of mind that the one suffering is caught in.

It is important to understand that if one truly wants to come out of suffering completely, help is needed from one who rests in *still mind* or *no mind*.[2] What truly matters for each and all, however, is that a start is made and not to be concerned about

---

[2] Still mind and no-mind are one and the same.

how it all comes together, for what is needed will manifest at just the right time. As the spiritual view broadens, what needs to be seen is much clearer and what needs to be done is understood without question. Just as one at the foot of the mountain cannot see at a distance and lives assuming that the view around him is the end all — the one who dares to climb higher, toiling without complaint night and day, has a much more expansive view of the play of the universe — and as the view expands, the constricted conditions under which one was living begin to lose their hold. Like the very first breath of fresh air is the feeling that comes when this expanded consciousness is experienced in its purity.

The Path to the One Heart

We speak of nothing, but I hear you

You call me by name as the wind sings

through the trees

You call me by name at the foot of the mountain,

the snowy peak stretched towards heaven

against a blue, blue sky

You call me by name in the mantra and in the holy

sound Om.

How did you find me here?

I heard you call me in the bustling crowd

with many voices speaking at once

At work with the sick and dying, there is your voice

You motioned to me as the tulip closed up at dusk

and swayed to the music of the sun at noon

In sleep, you love me as the bumblebee loves

the open flower, sweet with nectar

As the heavens meet the earth and become inseparable,

this is your voice… this is the meeting of you and I

The red apple so sweet to the tongue is made much

sweeter with the taste of you

You are the sustenance of my love

You sing to me wherever I look

You have made the darkness warm

and aloneness full

See now what I have become

The way of true spirit

See now how this form is too small to

hold you

and you are far too big and reaching to contain

only me

What is this I need to hear?

You have my undivided attention

This is the ointment

This is the one song in all songs

The unsung

The singer

The silence

You call my name

Part I:
Pure Caring

Chapter 1

The Experience of Pure Caring

When we walk into a patient's home, sit by a bedside of a loved one and hold a hand, place a cool cloth on the brow or listen to the words that pass from the lips of a declining or ill one, there is no need to be thinking about ourselves at all... sitting in this way leaves nothing to protect... simply the presence of being remains — in the moment, as it is, *nothing added, nothing taken away* — only the solitary richness of presence in and of itself. This is the experience of pure caring.

Boundaries

Boundaries are the ego's attempt at self-protection.[3] Who are we walling in? Our self — a self that speaks well of others at times then turns, oftentimes without cause or provocation, and speaks ill of others and the world. It is this same self that seeks to preserve the momentum of opposition, which brings in its

---

[3] There is a differentiation between external boundaries that are beneficial for safety and privacy and internal boundaries that are self-serving, protecting the heart and ego leading to further suffering, grasping and isolation. The boundaries being spoken of here are internal, self-imposed boundaries.

wake brief periods of joy, struggle, depression and mundane consciousness. It is this self that seeks protection through creating boundaries.

There is so much talk of boundaries in the healing world. There is talk of separating *my* pain as a caregiver/healer from the patient/client's pain. With this in mind there is a pull away from seeing the situation clearly. Most want to own their pain, to cling to it, pull it apart from whatever is occurring so they are not lost in the moment, lost in the heart and eyes of the other — losing oneself in this way leaves no pain to protect. Yet protecting what is called our own pain solidifies it, encloses it, pulls it in front of the vulnerable heart center where life beats easily and makes no distinction between you and I. To live in the heart is to risk being vulnerable. Most assume this means more pain, which is simply not true.

> *The river turns not one away from its shores that are in search of a bit of refreshment*
>
> *The one that takes time to kneel by its lovely gurgle*
>
> *and dip the hand in, conscious of the cool*
>
> *as it runs through each crevice*
>
> *It gives not a thought to who you are*
>
> *or from where you came*
>
> *Sit or walk by -*
>
> *it makes no difference*

None are excluded

Such a feeling when

the thirst is quenched this way

Vulnerability

Vulnerability is soft. It is flexible. It is yielding. The experience of vulnerability in its purity is only something most have a concept about. The concept automatically brings the feeling of being open to danger, followed by an automatic reaction to protect something that might be hurt. This is where the problem lies; the mind wants to stop short here, continuing on a cycle of fear of being exposed and then grasping immediately at self-protection, nothing but a wheel of pain, self-perpetuated, spinning itself for lifetimes on its own momentum. So vicious is this cycle, so continuous is its spin, that few barely get a peek at the mind suspended — where there are no concerns for a moment about the self. This is rarely, if ever, experienced. So there is nothing to compare and it is taken for granted that this continuous movement of mind is just the way life is… this is not true.

Do you ever stop to question, *What is this entity that feels it is in need of protection? Exactly what is it? What is this 'me' that is in need of protection?*

Pure vulnerability is an openness that is not of mind. It is that point where the mind is suspended — not concerned about itself, not preoccupied with the patient's troubles either. It is pure consciousness — whole, complete, moving of its own accord, taking care of itself, spinning the story, but remaining in the background, untouched, untainted, taking care of everything completely as it arises. Pure vulnerability is not open to danger. Danger that is mind made cannot touch it for it is the light beyond selfish desire. The best protection then is a quiet mind that has quit the ups and downs of grasping at a self-image and seeking internal shelter. The mind immersed in quietude is not vulnerable to the emotional roller coaster that ego offers up and is not tempted by it either.

Breath

When the mind slows, the world takes on a very different quality. This can happen with just a few conscious breaths. None really want to suffer, but most are too afraid to look deeper, afraid to take a chance. What is it that you might lose? The wheel of pain might stop spinning for a moment and over time eventually grind to a halt for good. Pain is not a very valuable treasure to give up. This makes sense logically, but we continue to behave illogically by clinging to it. Why? If you are truly interested in knowing, ask yourself the question and let the answer come on its own. Some insights may be revealed that surprise you.

Just breathe...

If you would try for just a moment to take a breath... slow down... not worry about the next step, you may be surprised to find you are right in step, right in step with the other. The tear gliding down the wrinkled cheek is your tear. The joy expressed when speaking of grandchildren, old times, travels, past loves — this is your joy. And the sadness, too — the losses … of children … of time... of physical health … of freedom of movement... all is yours. How can there be a difference? How can there be a differentiation between my pain and yours? Who tells us this story? This is the question.

Void of all distinctions

The heart of the divine mother is pure

In leaving ourselves out of the picture, we find we *are* the whole picture and how rich the picture is! Instead of just being someone that is looking to grow, protect, to help and so on, there is this potential experience of expansion, an expansion that can only be revealed when we give up the energy used to isolate ourselves from the other. This is the experience of selflessness and this is the experience of pure caring. Pure caring comes from a sense of being cared for, a faith that all is as it should be, that all is moving as it should. It is a knowing that the universe is inherently loving and loves in and of itself, as the flower, which gives of its fragrance. This is pure caring. It is one with the moment, beautiful, intact, yet not self-conscious. In this selfless state of being, the internal division between caregiver and patient falls away and there is only a substantial presence of caring and being cared for as the moment is taking care of itself in every aspect.

Light and Shadow

Light and shadow are experiences churned up by the cyclic movement[4] of mind and are nothing but mental attachments that continue to be held onto and built upon becoming distorted over time and having no relation to the truth.

Shadow cannot exist without light. Shadow appears when there is a holding pattern, which creates a dense field that cannot be penetrated by the light of the sun (the truth). This is ego — a weighted feeling or a sense of being a solid self. The more we are attracted to the shadow, the more it holds fast. Truly the shadow is nothing but consciousness bound by clinging, yet light continues in all directions, like the sun. This same experience can be seen daily played out in nature, and as we bring the attention to nature, it is understood immediately that the shadow has no substance. We don't identify with it. We are not afraid of it. But it is how much we make of the shadow side when looking at the psyche. How much energy is placed there! Sometimes it is even worn as a badge of courage. *Oh, how much I have suffered*

---

[4] Cyclic movement is inherent in the process of self-transformation.

and am still standing. I have been so mistreated in childhood. How hard everything has been.

There are experiences that have hurt us, this cannot be denied, but maturity means just that — growth, a different perspective, a movement away from, a casting aside of the old. Painful memories that have been carried over deny us the natural process of maturity and also prevent what is real from being known. Reality lives in the present without shades of black and white. It is void of mental colorings that appear as a result of personal experience Reality is impersonal — not in a cold way as if something has turned its back, but rich with life, unaffected by cause and effect, unconcerned about what just happened and what is to come. When the mind stills, this presence that has always been, makes itself known. It is at this time that the burden of being a separate entity, with its resultant suffering, falls away. Life presents itself in all its glory — impersonal, yet fluid, rich and deeply beautiful.

There need not be a movement away or towards

just a deep relaxing into the moment

Hold the self present

and do not run away from the light

In putting energy into the shadow

the psyche feels it to be alive

and fuelled with power

Yet it is illusive,

Powerless,

insubstantial

and always changing

Light does not need shadow to manifest;

it is eternal illumination

Inherent intelligence

unchanging

always

and everywhere

It is a very real way of being

It is enlightenment

It is Buddha

It is the Christ

You are now totally infused

with this light

Step out of the shadows

so the eyes may see

Resistance

To lose the battle of resistance is a very large victory; let the self be exhausted by it, tired of it, wiped out and fed up with it so that one can be pulled into the pure life stream which will bring new experiences of a deeper dimension. Nature will move in her course and help to clean out all the collected debris of the past, leaving a more expanded vision — then the state of things can begin to turn.

Sadhana (spiritual effort) is the bridge or raft that one uses to get to the other shore, the other reality that one sooner or later will be carried into, so to get to know this new land now is an intelligent move, a move that can only benefit oneself and others.

* * *

Pam

There was a patient I worked with in Hospice named Pam. After Pam died, all of the nurses, including myself, felt like it was the most difficult death we had witnessed: incessant clinging, fighting, sweating, begging, calling out... This behavior went on and on for days in spite of all comfort interventions — a very difficult process to be with. There would be points where Pam would relax, her breathing would settle briefly, but then she would jerk herself awake, so afraid to rest in the next reality that was waiting, to settle down into the hands of

God so ready to pick her up and wash away the past, but she would not give in and she kept on this way, exhausting herself and still kept going… amazing to see. Towards the end of Pam's process she relaxed a little with the help of some energy work, a little window appeared. It was a blessing to feel a brief quiet about her, a brief surrender.

* * *

The example of Pam is resistance that has come to its full fruition: the fighting, the pushing back, the struggling upstream, the calling out against a reality that has never been explored, a reality that one has never taken time to look at, to be with, to sink into. There has only been a floating on the surface, a rushing away or an exhausted paddling against the life stream, the eyes all the while looking for safety, always looking ahead or behind. Of course Pam lost this battle and in the losing is better off for it as she is out of the suffering of attachment to a fevered mind, of clinging to a very ill body. She is out of it for now and will have a chance to pick up again fresh where she left off. By the mercy of God there is another chance... and yet another chance.

To go on resisting without asking, *What is it that is being resisted? Who is resisting? Why this resistance?* If one is resistant to exploring further, inwardly ask, *Why?* Let the question sink and settle. Don't answer it intellectually — consciousness will bring the chunks of mental holdings to the surface very well on its own to be viewed. As one sinks deeper into the depths of consciousness, at first what is viewed is usually not such a pretty sight. This is normal as one is just beginning to penetrate the very hardened surface of mind. The initial surface is the most calcified layer, so if one feels drawn, there is a softer surface under the hardened cover which can be more emotional — there is an ache, an emptiness, a sorrow... and so keep going... and going. Let each layer fall away, warmed by the heat of loving desire, a desire to know the center of being.

As one continues in exploration, resistance will come up again and again (another very normal occurrence). Self-defeating thoughts[5] are ego's attempt to pull one back into the illusive safety of self-centered mental activity. It is the strong force that wants to suck one back into the endless whirlpool of mind that has become so familiar. To continue forward takes fortitude, determination, a faith in God that lights up the darkness, a trust that casts a steady beam of light through the thickened fog.

Resistance is an opportunity to see where one has gotten stuck. To be able to see resistance is a blessing because, by witnessing this play of push-pull, one is given a chance to move to a different level of being, a level that is more aware of self-defeating patterns. Fear of the unknown is what creates such a strong pushing force to mind and so to begin to explore just what is being walled out is a very intelligent move. Letting a little light in at a time is okay — a little time to breathe and be present... five minutes... ten... fifteen... can make all the

---

[5] The self-defeating thoughts and mental habits that comprise resistance can, to varying degrees, rest out of one's awareness — spiritual practice offers a light to help one see what is there and through this *seeing* a greater understanding comes as to how collected mental formations influence one on a daily basis and keep one from exploring the deeper levels of existence.

difference. To know oneself there needs to be a direct experiencing, not a lukewarm wondering or a pondering, reflection or concept — these risings of the personal view will never do. Just as when one takes the first bite of an apple, the experience blows out all thought of apples — so why talk when one can eat? The truth is that one can eat of eternity, but holds it away and settles for the insubstantial food of the transient — a shame because the apple is ever ready to pick and enjoy.

Denial

Denial is:

- *the disbelief in the existence or reality of a thing*
- *to refuse to grant (a claim, request etc...)*
- *to repudiate*
- *to refrain from the gratification of one's desires*
- *refusal to accept*

* * *

Alice

When I was still in training at the Hospice, I went out on one of my first visits with a bath aide or a staff member that does the hard, wonderful work of delivering personal care for the patients. Her name was Alice. One day Alice and I walked into this very large, well-kept home. We were ushered into the parlour by the patient's wife, Louise. This woman seemed to be in a hurry — she moved briskly, not really looking at what was around her. She quickly told us that her husband was receiving the last rites or the anointing of the sick by a priest. She sat us down on a long bench, went into another room and shut the door.

Alice and I waited for a long time. We could hear mumbled talking coming from the room. We waited and waited, with a nice long period to observe the pictures of family members on the wall and the perfectly tidy home with everything neat and in its place. Finally, Louise opened the door to the room, the priest walked out and left, and Alice and I entered the space. I had seen very few dead bodies up to this point in my nursing career, but it was obvious from the look of things that this man had expired. Alice and I looked at each other. Of course we were expecting a living body, as it appeared everyone else present was treating this gentleman as such. So, we just stood there for a while, at a loss for words. Louise was out busying herself in the living room. When Louise came back in the room, she looked at us blankly and as easily as we could, we broke the news that her husband was dead. She looked at us with such disbelief… and then the same look she previously wore returned. She didn't say much to us, I recall, but just went about busying herself in the house. There were no questions asked, no attempt to really look at what was in front of her. Alice and I put a clean shirt on the body and cleaned it up. The body was extremely stiff as if rigor mortis had set in hours ago.

* * *

When there is no urge to defend someone

or something

When this urge dies

True love blooms

Denial is a very heavy defense mechanism. Its purpose being to wall out what is not yet ready to be seen. There are many different levels of denial. In some cases denial is situation dependent, remaining intact for a certain period of time and breaking down when that situation dissolves. "I was certain he would live forever," one daughter said after her father's passing. When life has left the physical being of the patient, denial begins to break down as the loved ones can no longer tell themselves that dad is not ill — he will be getting better soon — that he is not dying.

Just as nature is in various stages of development — the seed, the bud, the blossom and the falling away, decay and new growth — so is the soul. There are situations in which a person is just not ready to *see*, and to attempt to push someone beyond this point is like forcing the bud to bloom at your command. It is just not time. Some information needs to be given, some feelings need to be expressed — this is fine, but it is best to deliver messages in the spirit of detachment and not be concerned how the other accepts it and then let it go. The daughter in denial up until that very last moment when the life force left the body of her father was not hearing what she was told — that her dad had just hours to survive. She wasn't going to believe what was said until the *experience* of it came to her. So it was best to give her some facts, but not attempt to change her viewpoint. She needed to see it for herself.

The other case of denial is very deep, more prevalent and not dependent on a particular situation, but carried over into every moment of existence. It is the cover that separates oneself from the natural state of the eternal bliss of God-union. It is the voice that keeps reeling us outside of our true self into mundane consciousness so that we don't have to look deeper at our present state. This condition of denial is what is typically brought to the bedside when we are caring for another and it is this state of mind that objectifies the other, pushes the picture away as if the environment is not related to the self. This type of denial is more serious because it has grown in and around the soft heart center for years and lifetimes. The remedy for this predicament is sincere spiritual effort infused with love, which uses far less energy and brings relatively quick relief compared to the energy and time put in to holding the illusion of denial in place.

It is very important to use the richness of experience as food for soul work, and caring for another human being is probably the richest heart-opening work there is. To begin to *see...* to know that one has caught oneself in a web of denial, that one is aching, that one is no different than the poor guy lying in front of him; these are realizations that if allowed entry, can begin the work of breaking down barriers held in consciousness and thus begin the important work of clearing the spiritual vision. This soul work, over time, brings a greater connection to the universe. It brings a feeling of unity, a sense of interdependence, a sense of wonder and awe and eventually, if one continues forward, it opens one up to the great mystery and richness of the universe — an experience that cannot be expressed in words as it transcends any other transient pleasure and experience of beauty ever known.

Doership

"We attempt to develop 'godly' qualities, thinking that God and self are separations and instead of coming closer to the ideal, we set up more separations. When you are not attempting to be better, nor attempting to change something, nor attempting to do, you simply rest within the fact that God is in control and always has been." — Swami-G

Doership is the weighted feeling of being separate from the universe. It brings a sense that we are our actions. This feeling comes from attachment to a self-image and an acceptance that the fruits of all action (be it pleasurable or painful) are ours. This is what creates karma — a continual playing out of the consequences of so-called "good" and "bad" action. It is ego that personalizes action and continues to keep the wheel of karma in motion. Ego is that isolated sense of self felt heavy in the head and heart. Fuelled by self-concern and self-interest, it is this entity that pronounces "I" and from there spins a separate, imaginary universe that is taken to be real. *I did a good job, I am healing this person, I am helping them to feel better.* This sense of doership is based on mind only and denies the universal treasures of healing, peace, bliss and love access to the heart center. It also brings with it a wake of shifting emotional states and a continual grasping at the self due to its unstable state. To stop and question, *"Who is doing?"* and *"What is this self that feels she is doing this or that?"* is called self-inquiry. Ask the question and leave the answer alone. The self cannot be truly brought out and spoken of; there is no substance to it.

Feeding doership creates a very narrow field of consciousness. It holds the focus on the personal self.

Karma

For every action there is an equal and opposite reaction.

Karma (which means *action* in Sanskrit) has a binding effect, holding one to a predetermined course and keeping the cycle of pleasure and pain in motion. It is not the action in itself that binds, but the sense of mental attachment to the doing. This attachment, or sense of being the doer, plays out in literally every action no matter how insignificant, creating an impression or seed in consciousness that, in the right conditions, blooms and brings the experience of pleasure or pain back to the experiencer. To check further growth of this cycle, one should go about activities with a spirit of detachment or non-involvement.

Detachment is a very difficult state to achieve and, as one continues forward, further assistance will be needed at some point from a spiritual master. A start can be made, however, by beginning to perform actions without attaching to the outcome. One can also perform duties as an offering to God. Even if one is not thoroughly convinced that God is the true power behind all activities due to having no experience in this way, this idea can be nourished in the heart and mind. Witnessing action, rather than being involved in it, can check the growth of new seeds of karma. Also, loving devotion to God is like a fire that can burn the seeds of karma, destroying them, leaving them unable to bloom. Keeping the heart open no matter what experience is manifesting aids in maintaining a calm, equanimous mind. Spiritual work takes self-discipline, a balance between vigilance and relaxation, a willingness to be honest and transparent and a strong desire to be free of whatever binds. Spiritual work takes time, and to begin one needs to have the desire and just take a step.

Free Will and Destiny

The "jiva" or "individual soul" is bound by the three malas (or roots): maya (illusion), karma (cause and effect) and anava (veil of duality), which, for an indefinite period of time, enshrouds the soul in darkness, thus obscuring the natural wisdom and light existing in the universe and allowing for spiritual ignorance. The condition of the jiva is not a permanent one, it is subject to changing conditions, and, like the shell of a seed that ripens and falls away in the right season, so can the shell of ignorance ripen, decay, dry up, turn to dust and blow away under the right conditions. The individual soul lives in the throes of choice (which is really God's mercy giving all a new opportunity at every turn of the road).

Personal responsibility for action plays a huge part in the maturing process and because by the grace of God there exists freedom to mature, freedom to remain stuck, freedom to move ahead or move backwards, the natural law of karma that blooms in the present moment is potentially fluid, so there is always room to shift. Still, the pull of the three malas on the jiva is very strong. This is why spiritual practice is so imperative. Righteous action, surrender to the will of God, spending time being quiet, listening to the longing of the soul, doing good works without attaching to the fruits, offering all fruits to God (which does not mean giving up all possessions, but rather an *internal* giving up), surrendering to the pull of the universe, getting the personal self out of the way, observing, witnessing, having patience, waiting and watching and then, by the wondrous unfolding of the universe, what needs to show up will be there right when you are ready to take that next step.

Non-attachment and Witness State

Vairagya: *Sanskrit word for non-attachment, dispassion, renunciation*

Unfortunately, the spirit of vairagya is poorly understood. Many equate non-attachment with loss, coldness, pushing away, lacking true love and isolation. The misunderstanding that surrounds non-attachment and the unwillingness to let go of these misconceptions are very much blocks to spiritual opening. The truth is that ego (attachment to mind and body) is the entity that associates with the presumed isolated states of lack. True detachment brings exactly the opposite. To renounce spiritually is to give up the pleasures and pains of the material world, which does not mean one becomes aloof and stiff like some robot void of emotion; this is the misconception. To be detached does not mean one does not love, it does not mean one hides away internally or physically, it does not mean one is manipulated or lacks preferences. These concepts are a continued expression of collective misunderstanding that keeps so many souls bound to a predetermined way of living and behaving in the world (Global Karma) which is, to be quite frank, more robotic — although it does not always appear that way from the outside.

It is fear (of the unknown) that holds the mind tight to mental constructions, pulling the soul back from the warmth of the sun (truth) that has the capacity to shine a light on the collected false constructs of mind so as to reveal their true nature. The light of awareness does the work of providing clarity to the mind simply by illuminating what has been pushed out of awareness. All that is needed is to *see* what is there, just look — without pulling back, without covering over, without running ahead, without creating something from nothing. The light of awareness does the work of opening and revealing in an effortless manner similar to the effects of the sun on nature. When there is no resistance offered, what is ready to bloom does so and what is transitioning and hanging on by a thread lets go as a healthy part of the process. To look without judgment is to be aware without resistance so the process of birth, decay, death and rebirth can move smoothly and bring one to a higher level of consciousness, a greater level of vibration. As consciousness clears, awareness becomes more steady and penetrating; in a way it gets brighter, hotter and just as the morning mist evaporates in the heat of the noonday sun, the mist of illusion evaporates in the heat of pure awareness.

Vairagya is allowing the process of nature to take its course without interference so that there is movement instead of stagnation. When a thought or idea manifests and is followed with attachment, it links up like a chain to the next idea/thought/concept, hooking with the next and the next in an endless manner — this is the mind train — this is what creates a seemingly solid self image and personal isolated universe. One lives enmeshed in this world, looking out through the images that rise up and color the vision.

To become aware of the workings of mind is a very important first step, which takes a pulling back from mental activity — this is called "witnessing." Witnessing helps kick the process of detachment into motion. It is like participating fully in life, but there is also an awareness that one is observing. This creates the feeling of *two* — the observer and the object observed.[6]

Witness state brings a greater clarity to mind, the difference being that one is able to view mental processes without being so taken over and easily thrown off balance by the shifting states of thought and emotion which in turn drives action and runs the risk of one feeling totally out of control... because much of the time we don't want to behave or feel the way we do, but there is a powerlessness about it as the course of karma drives our behavior. This condition of powerlessness and lack of control that accompanies mental attachment is not a free state, but a bound one — such a predicament can only become clear by discontinuing involvement and taking a step back so that a more expansive view of what is truly taking place can be had.

Mostly, one is absorbed in mental activity and doesn't even know it — there is no awareness of it. That is how powerful the spell of maya (illusion) is. It is so powerful that one doesn't even know it is going on. So, to become aware, to pull back, to disentangle is a true method of beginning to see in what one is caught — and when awareness becomes acute enough to

---

[6] This feeling of two dissolves when samadhi or union is entered — witness state is just a very important step along the way.

penetrate the layers of mind, it will be seen that its activity is empty, lacking substance... the movement of mind is impotent, having no power in itself — just waves of energy patterns, whirlpools of energy moved by the force of belief that such activity is real, solid and held in place by clinging, desire and self-interest.

That one can witness speaks to the fact that we cannot be the thing witnessed, that there is a consciousness far greater than what is bound by matter.

The desire to know the true self percolates up from the absolute or pure essence, the pure knowing that can never leave the soul as it is the foundation of all life — it is the substance or ground of being. It follows that the natural pull of the universe is in the direction of its true essence. The soul is eternally seeking its essence — no matter how far away it appears to have strayed. The pull of the absolute is what brings forward the desire to know oneself. It is this divine pull that brings forth the longing, the feel that something is missing, the internal ache, the desire to be whole. What moves the course of the soul through to its center is love.

Love is the nourishment, the water for the dry intellect and heart, the replenishing. Spiritual practices such as detachment need to be mixed with love to prevent imbalances that arise from misunderstanding, which can create an aloofness, a withdrawal from the world, a coldness and all the while one may be affirming that they are quite spiritual, yet they are very far from it. Spirit does not retreat, but flows in harmony with life, enjoying the full play of phenomena in all its beauty and wonder, without being entangled by it. Each moment is savored to its fullest and then the next moment is enjoyed without the residue of the experience that just passed.

> *Sitting still*
>
> *observing breath*
>
> *shadows move*
>
> *a light flickers*
>
> *nothing held*
>
> *nothing to push away*
>
> *a Buddha smile*
>
> *appears*

The experience of flowing with life can only happen when one unhooks oneself from the past and stops being mesmerized with what may or may not take place in the future. Vairagya is this unhooking, and then one is pushed along by the life current which brings the sense that this world and personality we once took to be so solid is not so. Appearances take on more of a fluidity, as do the mental processes. This is the pure life stream moving through the mental, physical and subtle body, cleansing and purifying as it goes.

As this cleansing progresses, there come moments when the personhood is washed away completely, leaving the residue or ground of being exposed — pure life, empty yet filled with the constant steady play of dance, color and movement. The personal self is lost to this pure consciousness and there is no one to regret a thing as regrets are born of mind, just like all shifting states. There is only rest and abiding deep peace — an experience that cannot be described in words, so as the sages over time have relayed, this experience can only be described by "what it is not." The experience of being absorbed in the ocean of universal consciousness cannot ever be known by intellectual struggle — not ever. The experience is not one of love as in the sense that one has felt love before; it is not one of knowing, as the mind is empty. It is not one of seeing, as the physical vision makes no difference. It is not an experience connected with body and mind. This is why a light from the outside — a mahatma or great soul — is needed, at some point, to pull one out of the habit of relying on the mental happenings as a guide — a very subtle and insidious game of ego that will keep one moving in darkness for an indefinite period of time.

Vairagya is of spirit, not mind; it is of heart, not head; and witness is a tool to be used when entering the path. It is to be used with a sincere desire to come out of the darkness. It is to be used with a non-judgmental, open mind. It is to be used in a manner that welcomes life; not pushes it away. The spirit of vairagya brings a feeling of depth. Emotions flow from this depth in a pure or purer state.

Universal Love

Love that is unattached (universal love) includes personal love and transcends it as well, leaving a fullness that rejoices in itself.

The essence of universal love is not dependent on an object — which does not mean love diminishes in relation to loved ones; nothing can be further from the truth. The confusion that prevails in regard to detachment is that usually love is equated with mental preoccupation: "He or she is all I think about!" One assumes that if the mind is not taken over by thought of the love object then this means there is no love.

There are many forms of love and personal love is really a more reduced form of love in its purity. It is a form that is boiled down and mixed with personal desire and expectations, which makes it more unstable. The impersonal love that rises from vairagya is abiding, as it deeply understands and accepts the transient nature of things. It is inclusive, yet not dependent on externals. It gushes up when one is alone and there is no object present. It is the fountain of God's love and it is forever gushing forth, available to quench the thirst of any who dare to let go in order to receive its grace.

So, love cannot go anywhere. There is no need to be concerned that spiritual progress will take something away. Once experienced it will be known that vairagya deepens beauty and love and it will be known that this pure love is, and has always been, available. Pure love abides everlastingly in the heart of the divine mother. Creation is made of it, sings of it, is enlivened by it and it is because this love is unattached, it brings with it a sense of richness and depth, a feeling of devotion, beauty and gratitude. It brings a rejoicing for no reason.

Some people do amazing things

Me, I prefer to do nothing

The small buds have already appeared on
the tree outside my window
and it is still winter

The universe moves with grace
Controlling nothing, yet always reigning
supreme
It has no way, but always gets its way
It has no desire to love, but is love in and
of itself
It behaves according to conditions, but is
unaffected by conditions
It is detached from the coming and going
Yet comes and goes freely anywhere and at
anytime
It is not made of mind,
but mind relies on it to survive...
It cannot be contained,
but is the container
and the contained
It cares not whether something contains itself,
but
moves about all hard substances like a rocky

river

bed

making its way to the ocean

The rocks being of its nature... it is

unaffected

by substance

It is all substances

It is no substance

It stays the same no matter what happens

just shifts here and there

It changes places

It doesn't exert itself, but gets what needs

to be done...

done

Such is the way of non-doing

The bird's call comes out of nowhere

and leaves no trace to follow

the traffic outside sounds like the ocean

The sun is making an appearance though it

never went anywhere

I am here and that is all

Relying on everything this very moment

Yet doing nothing

Some people do amazing things

Achievements beyond imagination

Me, I prefer to do nothing

No need to exert myself

No need to become anything

Emptiness contains all

Transparency

The ego desires isolation. Truly it is like an abusive lover using every trick of deception to keep one in the shadows so that it can continue to harp on its theme of *me and mine*. The nature of a possessive relationship such as this is to be secretive, to be private, to pull away and remain hidden, to shut and lock the door so no one can see because if the door is open and light is allowed to enter, this entity will be called out, its true nature revealed — just like the man behind the curtain in *The Wizard of Oz*!

It will be revealed that this entity given so much power is impotent; it is no-thing. It is like mist rising and that is all, but then of course, with this revelation, one feels their world to be falling apart and yes, the hard shell will crack, the earth will move and there will be a transition, a feeling of having a foot in two worlds. This is the thawing out, the falling away of the illusive coverings as the universe reveals its rightful place at the center.

The spirit of transparency[7] is revealing. It doesn't move back readily into the impermeable substance that is created through the private world of self-serving thought. Instead, it allows for this substance to be revealed, to be brought out into

---

[7] To be transparent does not mean we need to tell every little detail about our lives, to go through and look at every wrong doing, to go back and sift through the holdings — no, this is not it at all. To be transparent is simply a willingness to be present and give up what needs to be given up. It is a willingness to share when this is asked of one or to look deeper at the self without resistance. An honest looking, this is really all, an allowing, a yielding, an open sharing in the moment as it comes up and then a letting go. It is so simple — nothing hidden... nothing hidden... like the clear glass... this is transparency.

the light. Transparency is honest. It is forgiving, non-judgmental, open and trusting — all the qualities that are *allowing*. It is of the nature that offers without embarrassment or shame, which does not mean that what is revealed is always beautiful, loving and perfect. What is revealed just *is* and nothing more.

Transparency is like the clear glass that reflects, but is in no way affected by what is reflected. Its translucency allows for light to shine through so that what is there can be seen. A willingness to be transparent is a very important quality in a spiritual aspirant as it allows for the private world to come to the surface so that it may be sloughed off. What is allowed to surface has a better chance of being transformed by the powers of the divine.

Step into deeper waters

Experience richer aspects of your soul nature

What is holding you back?

Surrender

"*Whatever comes, comes — whatever goes, goes. There is no need to worry about it.*"

— Elsa, 94-year-old patient on hospice services

The universe is always moving towards fulfilling itself.

Surrender is working in harmony with this natural pull.

Surrender is giving up, giving over. It is an innocent observation of the moment, a melting and merging into the situation without being caught up in it, a giving up of all self-interest with a desire to merge with the other. It is floating in the arms of the universe, being carried by the current, sinking to the depths of the quiet, letting down the guard so the universe can do its effortless work, allowing Mother Nature to sop one up like a biscuit in gravy. This is surrender.

The fabric of the universe is supreme intelligence and pure love — this cannot be lost as it is the make-up of all that is seen and unseen. Through surrender, the density of the ego becomes porous, allowing the light of the universe more room to play. Experiences take on more of an expansive quality — the world begins to look different, colors are brighter, sounds are louder, energy in the body is stronger — all part of the internal journey and the divine mother (kundalini) doing her good work at breaking down the solid center or personal self. Staying open to this grace is surrender.

Hospice work is extremely fertile ground for the heart-opening work of surrender. Grace is ever-present in the perception of helplessness or the lack of control families feel they have over the inevitable loss of the physical presence of a loved one. There is that point where the feel of "Thy will, not my will" is undeniable, as the dying process progresses of its own accord completely out of the hands of the loved ones who may be grasping to hang on.

Even if one has lived with eyes closed to the flow of natural forces up to this point (the spiritual vision not yet prepared to accept the blazing glow of grace within each and every experience regardless of how that experience presents on the outside), even if the life has been lived completely enclosed, not once looking within, there is no greater sense of vulnerability than at the time of death.

It is at this time that the power of Shakti (nature), the true one that has always carried out the work of creating, of offering up and taking away, the giver and the gift, the true power behind all thought and activity, the color, the dance, the coming and the going, the beautiful, the ugly, the birth, the death, the decay and rebirth — it is she who is so palpably evident at the bed of the dying and it is the shock that nothing is truly in our hands that has the potential to cut like a lightening bolt through the protected hearts present. Shakti brings in her wake an experience of being woken up from a very deep and long dream. If even for a moment this new charge is allowed to sit in the heart, a different momentum can begin, a new seed allowed to settle and be nurtured that can, with surrender, bloom later when the conditions are right and set one on a totally new course. Each and every experience is rich for this work, but often it is the shocks that really start one on the journey of soul searching.

To be with each experience in full is to drink the nectar of life rather than settle for the crumbs and it is this nectar that is rich with the nutrients needed for growth. Be it family members or staff that are present at times such as these, what is offered is to be fully present, to see oneself in the experience. *This body so ravaged by the forces of time is indeed my own, this feeling of helplessness to the forces of the universe is indeed deep within myself, this one aching at the bedside is the ache of the protected heart thawing out.* This is the process that is true for all. Just be with this presence of change, of powerlessness, of the mystery, of the journey that continues on. To be helpless is to give up control and make way for the higher power to fill the heart so full that it eventually pushes out thoughts of *me and mine*. It is not a helpless enabling, but a helpless empowering, an empowering of compassion that is of the universe and has nothing in mind at all, but simply gives of its own nature.

* * *

Tracy

A very tender story of surrender is the case of Tracy. Tracy was a young woman in her forties. When I arrived at Tracy's home, her family and friends greeted me and brought me into her room. Another nurse was present who was an expert at doing dressing changes as this particular case was supposed to be very involved in that way. Tracy was sitting up on her bed when we walked into the room. She smiled and said hello. A very heavy presence of sadness hung about her. We talked for a while, just getting acquainted with each other. Then she said, "You know, I knew" and I asked her what she meant by this. She replied, "I knew I had breast cancer and didn't tell anyone or do anything about it."

I remained quiet, letting her speak and she told me there were very obvious signs — large lumps and followed quickly by a disfiguring. She did not tell a doctor or her family. She did not tell a soul. She expressed guilt about this and a heavy sadness. Eventually when she did go to the doctors the cancer was so far advanced there was nothing that could be done. I told her that all is moving as it should, to try to relax and let go of the guilt, that there was no blame placed. Forgiveness was, understandably, a very difficult concept to absorb in her condition. There followed some quiet for a while and then we started the dressing change.

When Tracy took off her shirt, the wound seen made one ache to look at — both breasts were nearly decayed away leaving nothing but deeply raw, red skin. The skin on her entire torso was purple and blue, totally open and raw. The slightest touch of the gauze on her skin made her wince in pain even with strong pain medication. It was a very slow and tedious dressing change, stopping every few seconds so that she could try to breathe away the pain.

The next day I arrived again to change the dressing (the change needed to be done daily). The patient's husband and son were present. We sat and chatted a while at the kitchen table. Tracy was resting in the other room. What came out in the conversation was that the husband had never seen Tracy's wounds nor wanted to, which was a choice he made and there was no judgment on it as each has a different state of readiness. I told them both, however, that it would be wonderful if someone would assist me in doing the dressing change. It was felt that it would be less painful for Tracy with two people working. Her son announced immediately that he would be glad to offer himself in this way. This young man looked to be in his early twenties. He was very casually dressed, wearing work boots and jeans. We went into the room together and began the slow work of changing his mom's dressing. Tracy's son (we will call him "Tom") helped soak the bandages and we both very slowly peeled them away from her skin. I was able to hold up one end of the very long bandages while he peeled away the other end, which helped tremendously, so that no part of the bandage rested against her skin.

Slowly but surely the bandages were removed and Tracy's torso was revealed. It looked worse than the previous day — more raw and bleeding. Tom remained very steady throughout the entire experience, speaking to his mom gently and lovingly. Tracy's head bent down at the time that the wounds were bared in front of her son and she wept. Tom remained a loving presence and told his mom what a beautiful, loving mother she is and how much he loves her. Tracy stood up from a sitting position and they moved in as close as they could, embracing for some time. Tom told her of his love — a very tender, beautiful moment.

When Tom and I finished we both sat back down at the kitchen table. Tom got a beer and he was shaking a bit. He told me he had never seen anything like that before. I told him that by surrendering to the opportunity and remaining in the heart, he had given his mother the great gift of forgiveness and unconditional love. I was very impressed by this young man's courage.

I saw Tracy one more time before she passed away. She was sitting up in bed surrounded by friends and family. She looked a great deal more bright-eyed, more awake. One could see the soft beauty in her face. Her friends told me she was able to stay awake for a poetry reading the night before where all had a chance to say goodbye and that she had moments where she enjoyed herself and smiled. Tracy died a few days later. I heard that the pain medications had helped her to stay comfortable.

Intuition

> *Intuition is pure intellect without knowledge*
>
> *It is the seed in the center of mind*
>
> *As the fruit grows from the heart*
>
> *enclosing it with the product of its own blood*
>
> *so does the relative knowledge of mind*
>
> *grow from intuition*

While it is true that some education is needed to perform a specialized task in society, caregiving primarily operates on intuition and it is very much at work whether one is consciously aware of it or not. Intuition gives a nonverbal understanding of the picture immediately. This understanding — that is not of mind — presents itself moment to moment as the situation arises and takes shape. This clarity moves in relationship to the challenge, moving in closer when needed and backing off when needed to accommodate whatever is manifesting at the time. This movement, when working at its optimum, is perfectly balanced, like the moon and the tides, perfectly timed, like the turn of the seasons, perfectly harmonious and in union like the male and female energies symbolized in the yin yang.

Intuition is the rudder that guides the mind through the waters of experience. Likened to the bodhi mind or the awakened mind, which is mind that exists as a seed state or pure potential, intuition is intelligence paired down to its raw state. It offers a sense of what is occurring without the overlay of personalized judgment. Intuition is the central power behind all words, actions and thoughts — relative knowledge is a mere secondary occurrence and shines due to its inherent grace.

Knowledge gathered through the years of education is useful to a very small extent. What use is there in being concerned with it, as most of what needs to be known will come forward at the time. If something is not known due to lack of experience, then there are resources readily available to consult. We don't need to know everything about a problem intellectually to respond to a situation. The more we cling to gathered knowledge and funnel it into creating and sustaining a self-image, the further we move from responding completely to the one in need, and the further we move from the natural gift of instinctive knowing. Collected knowledge is a tool; it is not the power behind function, it is not the teacher, it is not wisdom nor can it stand alone... knowledge exists due to the light behind it.

What is Intuition?

Intuition gives the potential for action and mental processes to take place. It is like the blank piece of paper of which anything can be written on or like the light of the sun that brings life-giving elements and illuminates behavior and activity, but is not itself the driving force or cause of behavior. As the mind becomes more in tune with intuition, action becomes progressively more fluid, more spontaneous. Complete immersion of mind into the divine light of intuitive consciousness elevates action to its highest good, which is always for the greatest service of others.

Though intuition is not the cause of action, it must be noted that there could be no activity without it. Its all-knowing guidance serves one ceaselessly throughout the day, even with something as small as crossing the street or staying in the center of the aisle when walking. The physical senses do not do the work of guiding, but are mere tools meant only to serve this divine light.

The further one strays from the core (the light of intuition), the more activity and mental processes become skewed as movement becomes increasingly resistive, working against the flow and harmony of the universe.

Intuition has no cause. It is fully contained within itself.
There could be no life without it.

"I don't know"

How afraid we are to say, "I know nothing"? We don't know why night rolls in and sleep comes over us, we have no idea how the earth prepares itself for the coming season, why fruit tastes so sweet to the tongue. We don't know why the autumn breeze on the face makes one smile for no reason. We have no idea why newborn babes are so amazingly intelligent, how one breathes or how the body works at all.

Mind

Its energies are spent attempting to materialize that which is immaterial, to grasp what is beyond its clutches, to make solid that which is fluid, to make certain that which is a great mystery, to isolate that which is open, to personalize that which is impersonal, to create dark emotional states when love is the one and only — such are the workings of the self-centered nature of mind. The illusion it hatches out every second of the twenty-four-hour day needs the fuel of confirmation, which comes in the form of attention to continue its spinning. To say, "I am not sure; I don't know," to be puzzled, bewildered, to be a fool as one vacant, stops this creative force for a moment, opens the gate, concentrates the energies and there is a pause...

We don't know, we don't know. This is the truth.

To accept that one doesn't know is the beginning of wisdom.

Innocence

Concepts about the world are collected over time or rather notions are simply built upon each other. There is absolutely nothing new in a concept — all have been thought before, all have been strained over before, carved out and carried over. The child has not collected concepts so she moves unacquainted with the world and its ways, unsuspecting, unsuspicious. This is the living reality of innocence and it glows in the face of all experience, whatever that experience may be.

Innocence is pure awareness without content. The play of nature is in union with innocence — pure, blameless, lacking intent. Innocence is not of age; it is a way of being. It is the heart of the fruit. It is the merging of mind with pure love. It is the joy and wonder of pure experience and the fearless acceptance of the mystery.

To be innocent is the height of awareness

The fool in the Taoist/Zen sense is one who lives moment by moment, leaving behind the residue of past experience and enters fully into the present moment. The fool does not carry the baggage of collected knowledge or gathered attitudes about life — each moment is completely new, fresh and innocent. The heart of the fool is so completely pure and trusting that nothing can corrupt it. Though the fool may be taken advantage of, made fun of or deceived, the heart remains ever pure, open and without prejudice, like a very young child.

The fool runs headlong into life without a care, open-armed, breathing in the scent that is carried on the breeze from season to season, in full play with life, bounding with its merry flow. Innocent, but not ignorant. Ignorant only of the workings of selfish intention, living trust, living faith, being life itself.

The Whole in the Heart

There is a whole in the heart where all that enters
is forever changed
and even the tears of yesterday bloom into the rose,
the lilac and cherry blossom

There is a whole in the heart
where what has fallen behind comes forward
sheds its cover and is revealed
for what it truly is
sweet clarity

There is a whole in the heart where
the monk, the beggar, the sick, the creative,
the ugly and beautiful are the same
as the light burns the face and name to ash
and the heart is revealed for what it has always been
Without separation
and at perfect peace

There is a whole in the heart
that shows where you have come from
where you are going
and what has captured you for awhile
meanwhile the sun shines warm day and night
the sky is alive with color

and life flows in all its wonder

the child dances

and sleeps

the sun is there smiling

and will wait for all eternity

Kay

* * *

When I walked into her room, she was smiling, her eyes twinkling, her face aglow. "Well you look like you are having a good day, Kay," I said to her. "Every day is a beautiful day," she said in a manner that made one smile and feel the blessing of the moment, so sweet and precious. Her body was nothing but skin stretched across bones, little bird-like hands and wonderful wrinkles covering her. Kay had been bedridden a long time, totally dependent on others for her care. She did not have an easy time of it. There was pain with movement and bedsores. She needed to be fed and changed, yet her simple words and presence emanated a sweet surrender, a very gentle peace and acceptance.

I knew her just a short time. She died the very next day.

* * *

Everyday is a beautiful day.

Divine Vision

When we return to a place we lived in our childhood, we experience it very differently, this is because life experiences have worked on the consciousness in such a way that the environment takes on a different appearance. It is not the physical eyes that have changed, but the internal view. The more youthful view of the world has been integrated with the pleasant or unpleasant experiences that have been gathered in between. The environment can be just the same, but it is taken in differently and so it is not the physical senses that have created this internal world from which we look out, but it is the personalized vision — mental habits and attachment to objects of the senses... and it is the momentum of this force that is carried over and over into every phase of life.

It is mind that creates the world that we see and as mind begins to dissolve, the world loses the shadow of judgment, separation and personalization it once took on. All that moves appears related to the self and yet there is a pervading stillness as if submerged in a deep, clear pool — nothing feels separate, all is divine... all is God. There are no worries or reflections, no concerns about what might be lost or gained — only a sweet gentle flow, a beingness, a wholeness, a perfection. There is a heartfelt understanding that life is a miracle and all is grace. All is grace.

The spiritual view is through the heart. It springs from the eternal fountain of pure consciousness that is all intelligent, yet void of all distinctions. Living through the heart is of the highest form of yoga practice because it refreshes and brings life to every other spiritual practice. It brings nourishment to a practice that has grown dry due to relying on intellect alone; it is the smile, the warm fire, the push that urges us forward. Because we love and are loved — this is why we keep going.

To lose ourselves in the moment, to be lost in the eyes of a child, in the eyes of a loved one or patient, to be absorbed by the moment — this allows love to take over. To do our work with tender, loving care — be it washing dishes, sweeping the floor or tending to children and family... to nourish the seed of the divine in the mind and heart is to begin to treat every experience as divine — with care, with love, with patience, with awareness and little by little as the seed is watered in this way, there will be a blossoming. Like all things, the fruit comes to the one who prepares well for the harvest. Such is the blessing of heart-felt sadhana.

That forgiveness flows in a steady current from the heart is undeniably true, for there are endless opportunities, doorways and open passages that lead back home to that which one truly is and has always been.

Spiritual Endeavor

Pure truth has never denied its glory to any;
it simply cannot come in and through that which is covered.

Just as the soil needs tending for the coming season — the hard dirt being churned so it can absorb the sunlight and moisture so complete with nutrition for a good, healthy crop —

the heart and mind need continual tending. Questioning the self (self-enquiry) aids in softening the tough, accumulated surface layer built up from lifetimes of clinging and identifying with the transient nature of mind and body. *Who am I? Where do I come from? Where am I going? From where does thought arise? To where does thought return?* These are questions that direct the self inward, chewing on the tough layer that surrounds the fresh tissue of the heart, softening it, making it porous so that the light of truth can enter. If the earth is hardened, cracked and overgrown with decay from lack of care, the healing rays of the sun cannot be absorbed — yet it shines on still as it is ever-present and in no way changed by hardness or softness. The light of truth is the same — always available, always glowing, always pure, radiant and naturally containing life-giving elements.

Sadhana is a Sanskrit term meaning "dedication to an aim." Sadh means to bring about — it is the effort given with the aim of God realization. One continues to toil night and day, preparing the heart and mind for what is to come. Sadhana is the work put in to care for a heart and mind that have been neglected. It is the tending, the churning, the loving, the blood, the sweat, the tears and the joy of effort towards bringing fresh life back to the garden of the heart. The gate swings open easily in the cool spring breeze when the lock is pried free, the rolling green valley exposed, the wild flower, the bee moving from blossom to blossom, the scent of the budding rose in the air. Life, in its movement and purity, is exposed. The prying of the lock, the tending to the garden within the chamber of the spiritual heart, the effort, the picking oneself up and trying again — this is sadhana. The falling away of the burden of the illusion of separation from the ever-present life-giving forces of the universe is the flowering of spiritual endeavor. The flower comes on its own; we simply clear the way...

Spiritual effort is not to be done with a mindset of doership. Though one is making efforts, practice needs to be heart-centered, not driven by the intellect. Any and all progression that takes place on the spiritual path is due to grace. Of course it takes the heart of a warrior to continue forward but not in the sense of struggle, resistance and violence — more a steadfast determination, no matter what comes forward, as a challenge.

Surrender, unconditional love, letting go, forgiveness, trust, faith, devotion, listening to instruction from competent guides, humility, honesty, accepting help, receptivity — these are tools of the heart that manifest due to the unconditional love of the universe to aid one through the inward journey when one has made a sincere call for help. There is a choice presented at every turn of the road: pick up the same course of ego or slow down, take a breath and allow the heart to do its faithful work of creating a new passage. If followed, this passage leads one through the land of the mystic and ends the journey in the heart where it once began. When one lets go of resistance, this wondrous inner journey can pick up speed. The mystical experiences that arise lead to the understanding that all is grace.

As the mountain rises glorious in the distance

above the shadows and passing play

so has the unchanging beauty of truth risen in the heart

and remains steady

undying beauty

As two rivers meet in joy

losing all sense of separation

so has this soul lost the separate journey

dissolved in the blissful ocean of all

As the stars sparkle against a black velvet sky

so does the glow of God sparkle in all that passes

life eternally blooming

As the fragrance is to the flower

so does this beingness contain

indivisible perfection

beauty and truth

the petals are falling in the garden

silent

silent

Chapter 2

The Body/Mind

The Body

The body — a lantern for God's love

The body is the lantern through which the glow of God's love can shine. The source of this light does not lie within the physical form, but radiates from the center or spiritual heart and therefore does not lie within or without, but is of one light, shining on irrespective of form and matter.

The body exists for a very brief period of time and, like all things material, wears down, decays and falls away. As the body moves and behaves, there is attached to it the mistaken notion that *we are* this body. It is the belief that the body is *who* and *what* we are that creates and holds fast suffering and in turn, continued clinging that arises from self-doubt. Chronic self-doubt is born from a deep knowing that we have centered our entire existence around something that is sooner or later going.

The root of all anxiety stems from the wrong notion that we are that which is transient.

The body is the artistic expression of God.

Merging the entire being into the present moment is like an offering or a giving of praise to the true artist — the true creator, that has brought the privilege of being in form so that one may have a chance to realize the joy of one's true nature.

The body comes into manifestation due to numerous conditions coming together at one time. It comes into being because of something else. It does not bring life to itself and cannot stand alone. Only the nature of the body can be known, but the moment-to-moment workings of it are a mystery. The body gives one a chance to experience. Like a vehicle, it only helps one move from place to place and experience life on this plane. It is a temporary dwelling for the soul. Being in body gives one a chance to pick up on the work done in past lives... it grounds consciousness so that life lessons can be seen, felt and potentially worked through again. That one has a body is a miracle. It is an opportunity to move forward into universal consciousness or at least expand the previous view which in turn aids humanity in moving out of mundane consciousness and into a more expanded, unified way of being.

Though it feels as if the body has a life of its own and moves about as a separate entity, it does not — it is neutral, moved by the force of mind...

As the body goes about its various functions there is a presence that is fully intact regardless of the experience. There is a presence that is witnessing the action of the body, but not of it. This presence is pure awareness. Like consciousness, pure awareness is a constant, it continues without interruption. It is persistent, steadfast and faithful. It is a presence that remains unchanged under any conditions. It is this universal intelligence or consciousness that remains after the falling away of the physical covering (the body) and consciousness exists prior to manifestation of form. Consciousness, like an element, cannot be separated into substances of other kinds. It is solitary. Though pure consciousness can reflect the holdings of mind, it is in no way bound or contaminated by the contents; however, these contents cast a temporary shadow over the pure light of truth and give the illusion of a more darkened, isolated existence.

It is through heartfelt devotion to God that the pure form of consciousness that stands distinct from mind and body (the atman or universal soul) can be revealed. Like a glass of clear water that has become muddied by holdings contained therein, sincere love of God and a strong desire to do his good works shine a light on the contents, which have manifested due to false views, selfish thoughts, self-serving action, attachment to worldly pleasures, craving for personal pleasure and the like.

The light of awareness is all that is needed to change the contents, wear them down, thin them out. Over time, with continued efforts, the holdings in consciousness become diluted as the pure light of awareness shines on day and night and eventually these colorings or samsakaras (conditioned mental views from the past carried over to the present) are washed clean. The world takes on a completely different appearance when looking through a clear glass of water compared to one that has been darkened by its contents.

When attachment to form dissolves, the body continues on its course — moving in a fluid spontaneous fashion — the universe filling the heart and mind with its supreme intelligent light.

Just Shift

A very simple exercise when one is moving about in the world and notices that the focus is self-centered is to make a conscious shift to pure awareness. Just pay attention to body sensations without the overlay of judgment. If one is walking, pay attention to the soles of the feet as they make contact with the ground. Relax into the step without coloring the experience with your personal view. Flow in harmony with the experience. Breathe into the movement. Don't pull back from it. If one is driving, focus on the feel of the hands on the steering wheel. Merge with the experience as it moves and changes from moment to moment without distancing oneself from it. Ground into the experience. Breathe into the experience.

To be aware that one is constantly absorbed in self-centered activity is all that is needed to help make the shift. One has to see it first to be able to help themselves move away from it. Just shifting is a very simple activity. It gives the mind a different focus and stops the continual fuelling of its self-centered movement. It also helps to heighten the feel of resting in the constant presence of now. Shifting can easily be done when working with a patient/client/loved one. When the mind starts dwelling on self-centered patterns, come into the breath. Take a few conscious breaths. Relax into the presence of the experience. Is one sitting or standing? Is one speaking loud or soft? Is the temperature of the room cool or warm? Let awareness move about the experience without trapping it by thought. Relax into the breath again if one finds they are pulled back into mind. This exercise in no way hinders the flow of the interaction. One will hear what is said more clearly and respond more fully without the distraction and exhaustion of the continual strain at thought and projecting what the next move should be.

Interdependence

Interdependence — This is this way because that is that way

As one goes deeper within the internal journey, awareness automatically falls on the body and contemplates it, looks deeper at it. Many of the Buddhist meditations focus on contemplating each part of the body, going through the skin, the muscles, the organs and with this deeper looking into the body, there eventually comes the insight of interdependence — an understanding flashes that all is connected and it cannot be any other way.

The body is created out of and requires the universe and its life-giving forces to survive; its manifestation is due to something else. From here, the question arises: Being interdependent, how can the body stand alone and pronounce itself a separate entity? This understanding is like a flash or a shock that can, if allowed, begin to remove attachments from the mind — though the feeling may be brief — it is a spark of understanding... it is a beginning.

Nothing is lost.

The tree is present in the seed — a small package of love

loaded with potential…

the soft earth laying receptive and silent

yielding without a care of itself — nothing is lost.

Breaking through, a small green tendril, supple with newness

like the downy hair of a new born babe,

its feet not yet calloused with time.

The seed exists in the leaf as the leaf could not be without it

and yet there is an unconsciousness of its beauty…

with no thought of itself

nothing is lost

nothing is lost… all present in the one — relying on no-thing

the course of nature, of mother… holding all near… bringing all

up well

The graceful descent of the petal or leaf, like a spiral of color

It cares not whether the wind pushes at it

or if the air is still and warm, fresh with the scent of lilac.

All life bends easily towards the sun on a day such as this

opening up, letting go

nothing is lost

Ahhhh… the decay… the sharp smell… flaccid… shriveled…

powerless

Mother takes this in her arms, like a beautiful child

the change in form troubles her not, all is love

As the skeleton where once there was a form loses itself to the earth

All is richer for it, all is included in it

The soft silence of death, the giving up, the giving over — the breaking down

the sweet mother of life holding all dear, providing all

The quiet of nothingness — rich with pure love

Letting go

Letting all happen on its own

Nothing is lost

Mind is One

The process that brings the entity called ego into existence is a universal process. While individual thought, outlook, feeling and emotion are different for each depending on the varying conditions, the workings of mental processes, the construction and the materials used to hold the construct together are exactly the same for each and all. This is another example that clearly displays the interrelated workings of the universe, the oneness that is ever present.

Mental attachment is like the glue that bonds the personal view together and from this narrow stance comes the flood of emotions that form the peaks and valleys — the contrasting shadow and light, the dullness of mundane existence, the continual worry about loss, the brief flashes of joy, the ache, the grasping, the spirit of independence with its accompanying loneliness... the feeling of enclosure — such is the terrain when one chooses to walk solely in the private world.

The ego creates and sustains the appearance of a private journey, private thoughts, personal feelings, personal passions, personal loves, personal pain and joys — all of which, in its movement, appears and feels very real and separate. If we look a little closer at the mental processes that make up mind, it will be revealed that this entity that appears so constant and all encompassing is held together by a universal material, which is the product of self-centered activity. It makes no difference if one is a lawyer, doctor, beggar or sannyasi, when mind is active, it is the thought of *I* that draws all other forces of personhood to it like a magnet. It is this collection of personhood that becomes more fluid in sleep and gathers itself together as soon as waking consciousness appears. With the *I* thought fixed in place, there exists a pulling force that continuously draws all that is seen, heard and felt into the personalized vision, then, whatever comes through the instruments of the senses is pushed through a narrow field, rather than allowed to float, expand and dissipate.

Spiritual evolution brings unique experiences, but as the process is allowed to continue on through completion, the final result is the same — dissolution of the separate self into the ocean of pure consciousness, which is and has always been the abiding presence of beingness.

Mind is Fluid

As we continue to shine the light of awareness on mind, illuminating the body of holding that is present, what becomes clear is that mind is movement: thoughts come... thoughts go... desire floats in... cravings and emotions rise... fall... moving, changing, growing... birth, climax, degeneration, decay and dissipation... an excitement... a disappointment... a frustration... a shadow... a light... desire floats... desire moves and changes... all connected to "I." *I want... I don't want... I am worried about... Maybe I can... Maybe I can't... and what if I can't... that felt so good when... that felt terrible when... I don't want 'it' to happen again... I... I... I.* Sometimes, briefly, there are moments when mental processes are suspended, a floating, a void and then a scrambling to the illusion of safer ground, and mind is back at it again.

Mental processes move, change, swirl and blend from one concept to another, like a running stream or moving train. Its movement is like life: changing, becoming, dying away. It moves, curves and weaves, fluid in its course and the more we allow the inherent light of awareness to shine; it will become clear that the entity of *me* that was taken to be so real is not at all solid. It is simply moving energy patterns, rising and falling out of a deep ocean of silence like waves.

Awareness is the sun

Consciousness, the ocean

Mental rising and falling, the waves.

Chapter 3

Emotions

Emotions are not a problem in and of themselves. Emotions are potentially very cleansing to the soul, like a spring shower that clears the air, rinses away the dust and leaves all sparkling clean — like a fresh start. When the heart is open, when it is yielding, emotions are allowed to run their course without leaving a residue of bitterness, isolation and misunderstanding (dark states that enter due to mental clinging).

Mental attachment is what twists emotion into a harmful expression, which narrows and confines energy, divides it into *me and mine...* and under the right conditions, this trapped energy can explode. It is from this volatile state (a state that is blinding and lacks true awareness) that words, feelings and thoughts arise that seek to hurt and blame creating ripple effects within our being — causing ruminations and fantasies that seek to hurt, divide and reinforce the *me* story. It is this war of division within ourselves that must be looked at first before we can see anyone else clearly.

The mind has great power of creation — it is very potent. This power is not ours to manipulate as it can turn back around on us so easily. It is only with a broader view that the very potent energies present in the universe can be seen and honored.

One can start out very angry at another, yelling, lashing out and name-calling — yet often, as time goes on, there is a contemplation, a reflection — a little light is allowed to enter, a little surrender, a softening of the soul towards the heart. There is a giving up... a sadness... a sorrow... a wanting to forgive... a wanting to be forgiven... a melting down of the barriers... a love for the other... a little understanding. The very same energy that was distorted into rage is transformed into something much broader with surrender.

Awareness is like the lamp that sheds light on the workings of mind because without vision we are at the mercy of the very strong unpredictable forces of mind and thrown about in the whirlpool of this mixture.

Emotions in the Selfless State

When there is no "I" at the center, emotions come and go, moving with the uninterrupted flow of life, here for a moment and then gone. There is no hook, no *me* story that catches them, no personality in place that gathers them in and builds upon them. Emotions arising from this selfless state are simply spontaneous expressions, more like those of a very small child — there are tears and then done, with no trace of remembrance or feelings harbored, just an immersion into the next moment, an expressive unfolding of being that is doing just that: expressing, flowing, moving — each expression dissolving into the next, art in motion, poetry in motion, doing itself, being itself, no deep-rooted meaning to it, just flow... moving... moving... wandering... life...

In the pure (selfless) state there is sadness, there is happiness, there are disappointments, but not in a manner that is solid or continuous. To the observer, the one residing in pure consciousness may look serious, angry, surprised, stern or joyous, but internally, there is only a pervading stillness that is untouched by these externals... and because this one is out of attachment to the transient and lives in the deathless state where all is known — it is from this perspective, one has the long distance vision — the eternal vision — and can see that all is of the same essence, of the same fabric. Still, the jiva[8] clings to the shadows when this freedom is the birthright of all.

This is the compassion of a Sat Guru[9] — to remain and help when they themselves are not in need of assistance anymore. It is sad to say this, but very few accept the help, having no experience or understanding that there is another reality to be entered, which gives rise to freedom, thus, ending suffering. This is the way of the universe — always giving, giving, giving, inherently protective and open-armed. It is only the surrendered heart, the humble soul that can soak in this ever-

---

[8] Jiva: the individual soul bound by the three malas or roots — Maya (illusion), Karma (cause and effect), and Anava (veil of duality).

[9] Sat means true, absolute, eternal – a Sat Guru is a true Guru (an awakened one).

present beauty that leaves one completely vulnerable and open, yet completely loved and protected — dissolved of fears, dissolved of attachment to body and mind... complete... full... whole. Cleared of selfish desire through surrender, a Sat Guru, embodies the universal spirit. It is a gift — though very misunderstood as so many offerings of the universe are. The jiva thinks to himself, "There has to be a catch to this…" because for the jiva, the internal world of mine and yours, loss and gain, positive and negative, light and shadow, this struggle is all that is known, therefore anything outside of this view is distrusted. This is the narrow vision — what is outside of this view is sensed as an intrusion... so one is free to go on this way. Possibly, in just hearing that there is another way, a seed will be planted that, over a period of time, may ripen — this is the hope.

May the seed of eternity be nourished in each and every heart. This is the prayer that flows and abides everlastingly in the heart of the divine mother.

Stepping Back From Emotions

There is no need to be afraid of emotions. They rise from the ocean of consciousness like waves. When the winds of desire are strong, there is much more turbulence. When emotions appear to take over, come into the breath. There may be a stream of mental phenomena that accompanies the emotion, allow the stream to move without attaching to it. Slow down (this is very important). Speak slower. Breathe into the heart center. Take your time. There is no rush. Step out of the room, if necessary, for a moment. When possible, sit for awhile, allow the energy of emotion to rise, witness what comes forward... breathe... relax... go into the emotion... don't run from it... don't create a story out of it. If mind begins to create a story, just notice it. "It is just mind and mind is not *who* and *what* I am." Continue to come back to the breath. Allow the emotion to float... allow it to dissipate. Emotions in their purity are what they are… they come and go... they rise and fall. Stay steady in patience, steady in heart... open to the blessings that are always present in the moment.

Allow awareness to expand beyond the constrictions of the emotion... wider and wider... allow more light to enter. Afterwards, go about your routine slowly: *now I am sitting, now I am standing, now I am walking*. Come into the breath again and again. Notice if mind wants to go on and on about the experience — just notice it — "Isn't it interesting… mind keeps going." This is the work of spiritual practice: one step at a time. After a period of time, what your responsibility is in the matter will become clearer, but there is no point in struggling with it, in churning over the same ground. Let things settle. Come through the heart and what needs to be done will be known; what needs to be given up will fall away. This is the movement of the intelligent force of the universe, which is consciousness, ever present, giving in nature, being what it is — it can be nothing else. It is through heartfelt spiritual endeavor that this consciousness that is constant, this consciousness that is supportive, can move unobstructed and do the work of true healing.

Loneliness/Emptiness

Loneliness is your own being

knocking on the door to the higher self

asking to be made whole

Loneliness is a symptom that one has journeyed away from the core of being searching to find an experience that is lasting — an undying love… an unwavering bliss… a steady communion… a supportive presence… a union — this is the search that the lonely heart is on. There is no difference between one who is seeking the truth and one who seeks fulfillment outside of themselves[10] — the desire is the same. The one who seeks truth is simply ready and willing to give up looking for completion outside of themselves due to exhausting this path, having finally discovered that this method of seeking has no

---

[10] Some mistakenly think to let go of searching for fulfillment outside of themselves means one must live like a hermit, deny themselves of relationships or withdraw from family and loved ones — not true. Our family, our friends, our current situation in the moment as it is — IS sadhana. What is encouraged is to let go of and question the spin of personal desire to give one a chance to experience the moment in a fuller way. What is also encouraged is to notice how mind sabotages as well as denies the simplicity of the moment by constantly seeking something outside of itself.

lasting value, because though experiences have come that may have brought temporary happiness, the internal feeling of emptiness — an emptiness that is barren — eventually rises once again.

Loneliness is a beginning.

All who have embarked on a spiritual path had to start from the beginning like everyone else. The beginning is where you are at now. It is the present state. To sit with what is arising in the present moment is the only way to get a feel for what is being pushed away. The truth is that what is being pushed away is not what one thinks it is — so what is it? What is this emptiness?

There are times, when one is enjoying an experience, so absorbed in the moment that the individual self is forgotten. In these moments, there is only raw experience, not someone experiencing. What remains and is revealed in these moments are the inherent joy, rapture and deep beauty of beingness. The covering of separation (the personal self) has dropped for a moment exposing the pure life stream.

When you are not, life IS...

The experience of self-abandonment is termed "no-self" or emptiness in Buddhism. "No-self" does not mean that there is no existence, but rather, there is no inherent individual self. If one has ever experienced moments of self-abandonment, it can be described as anything but empty in the barren sense — it is a fullness that is rich and substantial. The moment is completely savored for what it is, there is a being in the moment, but not of it — a void, pure potential, true love, timelessness, still motion, free fall, silent witness — so many ways to describe this beautiful experience when *you* are not, but at the same time — life IS...

In the darkness of that night

With the chilling wind crashing
And harrowing cries of the wild
The floodgates spilled open
And all manners of demons sprang forth

In the Fortress of Being I rested
And watched as the wind became Still
The cries of the wild fell Silent
The flood waters now motionless
Holding the Reflection of the Rising Sun

Paradise Reborn

—Sage Sarojini

Fear

It is because so much resistance is given to this emotion (fear) that it offers the greatest potential for freedom when transcended. It is not fear that creates resistance — but resistance that creates the dreaded emotion we term fear.

Mental imagery and externalizations that accompany fear are richly symbolic and offer potential clues to childhood conditionings that have been habitually carried over and played out in an unconscious manner. Very common fears such as fear of the dark, fear of being alone, fear of intrusion and fear of loss of health and function are highly symbolic of mass mind's defense mechanism, which stems from insecurity and serves as a collective cover to higher consciousness.

As one looks deeper and gains clarity, what will be seen is that fear is a potential passage to another reality and arises again and again as an offering — to give one continuous opportunities to explore and move beyond it. Just as constricted energy that is held in place by mental attachment can transform into boundless awareness through the proper use of surrender, devotion, spiritual practices and love, the most dreaded mental state — fear — can be transformed in the same way. Quite often, fear is the last doorway one passes through on the journey to internal freedom... it is because so much resistance is given to this emotion that it offers the greatest potential for freedom when transcended. For example, the fear of the dark can open up to *the void from which all life springs* — fear of being alone (as well as fear of abandonment) can transform into the *aloneness that is empty, yet full — rich with all of life,* fear of intrusion can give way to *the breakthrough or break-in of Christ consciousness that emerges due to letting go of ego* — fear of loss of health and function (the fear that arises from the misunderstanding that consciousness is limited to mind and body) can dissolve into *an absolute knowing that one is not this body, not this mind, but everlasting spirit.*

The majority of fear has no base in reality; it is not brought on by anything outside of ourselves. It is not what one thinks it is (so very scary) — it is not what mind has made of it. It takes vision to see what is there, so one must not turn away. Stay and observe awhile... breathe into it... take a peek... take a breath... don't judge what it seen... just be with it... and as always... keep the heart for company.

Don't take it so personal.

Fear is not our natural state. The majority of anxiety and fear are irrational — nothing is occurring at the time to cause such a reaction. There is nothing happening at all — one is safe at the time, one is well fed, one is warm, one is breathing — there is just life moving, changing, this is all, yet anxiety surfaces and keeps resurfacing. Fear has its roots in the past, usually stemming from a time when one felt helpless, unprotected and unsafe. At this time there could have been something very real occurring that was dangerous and this created a very strong impression in the mind. Yet, even when no threat of danger has taken place for quite a long time, this feeling of being unsafe continues to rise in the chest. This is what needs to be seen — that the resurgence of this emotion stems from a replaying, a churning up, a reliving.

When there is a threat that what is so familiar may be taken away, that there may be a loss, there is fear — and what is so familiar is the internal world of *me and mine,* which consists of attachment to mind and body — *my body is me, my mind is me*... if this goes, then what remains? This is the deep root of fear, which stems from the misunderstanding that body and mind are all that we are. This misunderstanding is developed and solidified over time by clinging to narrow notions that what is seen is all there is, that something can only be this one way, that it can only be *my way* — when there is a perceived threat to this very sheltered world, there is anxiety.

Anxiety serves as an illusive and very painful defense mechanism against looking deeper at one's true state. Much of the time anxiety is generalized or it connects with an external event or situation. It can become obsessive — which is really just one swimming around in a very small whirlpool on the surface for fear of relaxing and sinking deeper. Irrational fear is an urge to protect the private world of *I,* the treasured world of *me* and *mine*. This is the crux of the matter as all anxiety stems from the fear of personal loss.

Certainly there are very difficult experiences in life, but still, each and every experience is *the human experience,* for there is not one that cannot recall something similar that they themselves or a friend is going through. Human experience is the common experience and if one can begin to view personal experience in more general terms, so much of the isolating feelings of sadness, loneliness and anxiety can be soothed somewhat. This is a beginning: not to cling so strongly to individual experience as if you are the only one. Your neighbor has many of the same stories — look around, listen... be quiet. One will hear the call of life in each and every experience, *the human experience* — the experience of living, growing, suffering, learning, letting go, trying again — all present in the one experience, all the same.

This is not to simplify suffering and anxiety — it feels very real — very externalized. This is not to simplify or belittle individual losses of which some have had more than their share, but there is a different perspective, a different view and if one is willing, there is something broader under the surface that can help to thin out the pain of individual holding. If one is willing to explore and move beyond the surface, it will be seen that there is nothing chaining one to past trauma. There is not one who is being forced to keep the images and thoughts running — to keep the wounds fresh. Attention is being held there by the collected concept of who you *think* you are — the personality, the individual. There is attention and there is a vigilance that none come and shake up these collected notions because then what — *what will happen to me then? What am I without these gathered concepts? Who am I?* This is the question to stop with and let settle. *Who am I?* Leave this question alone because it will do its own work... it will sink deep... it will draw up mental debris to be seen and cleared. *Who am I?*

The only threat is the personal self: the self against the self, the self defeating the self — the separation, the division, the personalities of the self — the company of the self, the good and bad selves, the angels and devils of the self — all split off from this entity of ego that proclaims *I*.

It is this internal world that is guarded and there is fear... there are *what ifs*. There is fear of intrusion, there is fear of a break in, of change, of uncertainty — there is doubt. This is because one has identified the self with the transient and the personal self is just that — transient: becoming, declining, dying, being reborn, hoping for something else, looking forward, looking back, moving, shifting, changing. There is no stable ground here, no anchor, no foundation, no true faith — just a hoping — *a longing* — to stop here is also good. Let this longing sing its song; let this ache throb away. Let it burn to the depths of the soul. Be quiet with it — allow it to burn the coverings that protect the soft tissue of the true heart — to bring new life to this place... and keep going until one can see clearly, until individual pain holds one no more as what is revealed is empty and the majesty of "true heart" — the "one heart" — can be embodied in all its glory.

a little sip of eternity goes a long way...

Even a brief glimpse of the universal soul makes every effort, every tear, every step on the path (no matter how rocky) worthwhile (and will also keep one charged for the many miles to come).

One needs to take a step to begin that long journey inward.

And when, my friend, will you begin?

Compassion

When I look through my eyes, I see someone looking back

When looking through the heart, there is nothing, but love

Allowing the heart to extend beyond the limitations that mind has imposed upon it, leaving room for another to enter —

this is compassion. Compassion sees suffering and knows it, having traversed this same ground at one time or another.

When there is no urge to fix something,

we can listen, be a spectator —

an honored guest in the play in which only God is the director.

When we sit with another, much of the time, we are seeing them through our personal history with its continuous projections, urges, joys and sorrows. When we sit with another preoccupied in this way, so much is missed — a true connection is missed, not a connection that is personal and self-serving, but something much richer — a universal connection.

When we personalize suffering,

we close out the suffering of others.

Most of the time all that is needed is a sense of being heard — this is felt by the other at a heart level — a connection, a synchronicity — something moving at a deeper level than intellectual.

The Compassion of Tough Love

When I first started meditating, I thought being spiritual meant being loving, kind and helping everybody. Since meeting my Guru, this "idea" I had about spirituality has changed from a concept to direct experience. My Guru has often said, "Being spiritual does not mean being a doormat." Refusing[11] to accept any nonsense thrown our way or refusing to perpetuate a debilitating situation is another movement of love as it does not support that which weakens us, another or humanity. With this statement, one can see that love can move in many ways and still be love.[12] In certain situations, by not supporting, by not speaking, we are helping by not adding to collective negativity. In other situations, love speaks out in a very direct manner and what is spoken is what needs to be said, not necessarily what one wants to hear.

True love risks all. It does not compromise the integrity of the whole.

---

[11] Though the word refuse is used here, it is not in the sense of doership. Pure love, which is the inherent compassion of the universe, moves by whatever means necessary to bring one in harmony with the universal life force. If the heart and mind are willful, chronically resistive, self-destructive in spite of encouragement to move away from danger, then the guide within cannot be heard or received and one is freed up to continue on in whatever direction they are drawn.

[12] The core of perfection is at the heart of all beings, this can never be denied — what is being denied, refused or spoken out against is the action — this is the movement of tough love in its pure state — it will not embrace or support activity that weakens.

Of course, what is being said or not said, may not be taken in — it may not be accepted into the heart, but the aim is always to give one a chance to see themselves more clearly — to grow, to mature, to open up. This may mean the "velvet hammer" or the "two by four" — terms my Guru also uses regularly.

Tough love does not mean we cut someone out of our hearts or nourish thoughts that divide, separate or seek to harm.

Tough love does not mean we love that person less or have given up. Tough love in the pure sense is a wake up call — like a shaking from the universe. Sometimes, people that are on a destructive course need to be left to their own devices because it becomes unproductive to continue on in a more intimate fashion. This is another way of helping someone to stand on their own feet — to look at themselves. The other may or may not take the opportunity handed to them. This is their choice.

Relationship is a reflecting glass to see ourselves clearer.
We can only see others through the screen of ourselves.

When negative thoughts arise, come back to the breath.
Don't entertain them.

We cannot save everybody.

To help transform others, we need to first look at ourselves.

Suffering

To resist is to suffer, to pull back, withdraw, hide away, tense up, shield the vision, assume, stay rooted in one spot, hold one perspective, divide, block, build walls and justify... to resist suffering 'is' suffering.

Suffering[13] is not inherent in direct experience — pain is not contained in the thing itself — it is the product or fruit of the divisive mental play of mind. It is the entity *me* that wants the fruit of the experience for itself — that wants to devour it, to enjoy it privately, *my gain, mine*! It is this personal outlook that indeed receives the rewards because one always gets what they are looking for. The other side of this *me* mentality is fear. There is fear that something will be taken and, as all things inevitably change, something in the personal field is eventually taken. Material things break down, wear down, transform and change — physical things are inevitably absorbed and taken.... and there is grief. To resist the inevitable, to resist the truth is suffering. To

---

[13] Suffering is defined as attachment to mind and body — the internal contradictions as well as restless moods and thoughts that flow out of grasping at a separate self.

create a fantasy world to shield one from reality is suffering. And this resistance, this dream world, is so very complex, so filled with struggle, weighed down by constantly balancing gains and losses: *What to do? How will I receive the best thing? 'I,' 'I,' 'I'...* when the truth is so simple, so very simple and subtle, so very close at hand that it gets missed.

What is this suffering? Stop and look at it. Go into it. Turn around and face it. This is the only way to catch a glimpse of what one is running from. What is it exactly that is keeping the mind in perpetual motion?

Suffering is God's way of waking us up

so he can show us the way home...

Every experience that comes is a potential teacher, which does not mean that there needs to be some deep, personal meaning to experience. There is something much more beautiful hidden in experience that is impersonal, yet extremely rich and substantial. To let go of personalizing experience and to begin to see with the divine eye... to have faith that there is something beyond individual emotions and clinging.... to let go of the notion that liberation will only come in some perceived heaven, some perceived thought about future... to have faith that liberation is at hand — that it is here and now.... to relax fully in the moment and in time, discover that one is held eternally in this great ocean of bliss that is totally impersonal, yet inherent, constant, intelligent, supportive, substantial, always... to begin now, to go into suffering with an open heart and mind, to know that what is captured by the senses is not it — to be present and fully enjoy the play of the moment, letting life move one, letting life become one, letting love capture one — until there is nothing other than... this love that is... this life that is... open and free.

The most difficult experiences can potentially bring the greatest growth if one remains open, yet one does not have to suffer. This is the call of the heart. There is no suffering when the illusive coverings of mind fall away. Suffering does not have to be; it is not inherent in us. It is not eternal. It is not natural. It is self-created and sustained.

When the *I* dissolves there is no personal attachment to experience — just flow. What comes, comes; what goes, goes. The universal soul remains, it is constant. If a loved one is passing, one knows they are really not going anywhere; just the physical covering is being shed. The heart of one, the love remains. This *is* faith — a living faith, a true faith that has become a reality due to direct experience. When the heart is entered and lived through, all experience is God — nothing else is. There *is* no other. Nothing and everything — all in one... the one heart.

* * *

Linda

Linda was 32 years old with a diagnosis of glioblastoma (brain tumor). It always grabs the heart when the admission paperwork reveals a young patient with small children. These admissions and nursing visits are very difficult and extremely sensitive.

Linda's husband, John, greeted me at the door. One could feel immediately that there was a heavy sorrow that hung over him. The energy of the house was extremely lonely, barren and heavy. John and I chatted awhile. He told me Linda was sleeping in the bedroom and has not responded at all for the last few days. She had not eaten or drank anything in days. He told me a little history about their lives: that after she was diagnosed, there was a six-month period (after receiving some treatment) when she felt well. During this time, the couple traveled, enjoyed regular activities and just lived their life. John told me that he never mentioned the cancer to her or ever spoke of the possibility of her dying, as he just wanted so to enjoy the time without spoiling it with this kind of discussion. The couple had two boys, ages three and five. John told me they were doing okay. (The boys were not present at the meeting). John said he did not speak to them about Linda's disease and they just grew accustomed to the way that things were, as the kids didn't know any different.

After we were done getting acquainted I asked to meet Linda. John opened the door to their room. At this point, I was not able to see Linda's face. She was lying on her side, away from me. I needed to check her lungs, skin and reposition her in bed. John helped me with this and we rolled her over. When we rolled Linda on her back, she did not respond, call out in pain or put up any struggle as the body was extremely relaxed and giving. Her face, when revealed, was very beautiful with translucent skin and she wore the most serene, peaceful smile that I had ever seen on a patient. She seemed to be in such deep peace, very withdrawn and removed from the external happenings. Her husband attempted to rouse her by calling her name. He even joked with her to try to bring her to his reality, but she remained in this blissful-looking state.

When we went into the front room to talk a little more, the sorrow that John was carrying and the loneliness of the house was so heavy, so palpable — a striking contrast to Linda's seemingly bliss-like reality. We talked about how peaceful Linda looked — there was nothing to be done except to get comfort medications for emergency use and a hospital bed to help keep her comfortable, but that she looked like she was doing quite fine. Hospice was also there to support him and his family. As I was leaving the home, some other family members were coming into the house and said to me, "You have the hardest job. I don't envy it." I didn't share this sentiment at all, but have always felt it is an honor to give support where needed. One felt empathy for the long journey John had before him, but Linda was not part of this struggle, as she seemed so completely surrendered and absorbed in the bliss of God's love.

Linda died peacefully two days later.

Our Struggle Will Till the Soil

The greatest fear is of myself

But Who am I?

When I look for myself

I find nothing that is separate from the universe

I can't find myself anywhere

Yet I find myself in everything

There is the flow of life

There is the simplicity of being

This ego thing is a phantom

I can't touch it or see it

I separate myself from others

by believing its lies — that I am different

I am of the same heart

God's mercy will show me this

and my suffering will be for the good of all

My tears will bring the dry bed of earth moisture

My struggle will churn the dirt making it rich to receive

My doubt will open the door to certainty

The illusion of separation will help me to recognize

the feeling of one

Surrender, sincerity, an open heart

This is the fertilizer

We do the work of tilling

God brings for the harvest

and when the work is done

there is just the harvest

that comes and comes...

Part II:
The Path to the One Heart

Chapter 4

Healing Touch

Energy Work and the Actively Dying

> *Death came for me today*
> *He was full*
> *of infinite mercy*
> *and filled with*
> *compassion*
> *He beckoned me forward*
> *and allowed*
> *me to pass*
> *into Eternal Life*
>   —Sage Sarojini

While it is true that profound spiritual cleansing can take place during the dying process, it is in one's best interest to spend the days now preparing for when this time comes — to enter into the moment with a heart of sacredness and gratitude, to begin a spiritual practice, to cultivate patience and understanding, to question what has been taken to be real. To humble the self to a divine being that can cut through the false notions and illusory holdings that maintain separation, slowly as the coverings fall away, it will be known that death only comes to the ego (to the *me* mentality) which once dissolved leaves pure spirit (eternal life).

My legs have become too weak

to run away

My mind too soft

to argue

I try to speak, but no

words come

I try to fight, but

have no strength left

All I can do is listen

Wait and

watch...

...now that I

have returned to the child

I have always been

I am ready to be held

When the dying process advances to its final stages and one has a few days, a few hours, a few minutes left to live, vulnerability is at its peak, which offers a precious window of opportunity for spiritual cleansing. The helplessness and vulnerability that presents at this stage can literally drench the heart and mind with the living waters of surrender and what has been hidden and struggled with an entire lifetime is brought effortlessly to the surface to finally be sloughed off. Not only are the heart and mind vulnerable at this stage, the body is totally helpless and as open to being touched as a newborn babe, for there is no voluntary control over the physical processes anymore.

The body, the mind, the heart are not as able to put up the same habitual wall of resistance in the actively dying stage. The senses are often more acute and this can be seen in the eyes of many actively dying — the spark of intelligence in their eyes is sharper than ever as they are picking up everything that is occurring around them. What lies before them is unknown and inwardly they are very much aware that a shift into a new reality can occur at any moment. Every minute is taken in like it is the last. This state of transition where all the faculties are heightened, keenly aware, and the state of mind is helpless yet giving, literally soak in the life giving forces of spiritual energy and there is the potential for great leaps in spiritual growth. The family is on edge during this stage as well, emotions are surface, more fluid, the entire life history comes forward and reveals itself. When the hearts of the family members are open and not entirely taken over by grief, a precious opportunity for healing is offered to them as well and large chunks of long held sorrow can potentially be cleared and resolved.

Energy work most importantly helps the patient to relax and shift away from body identification into resting in the supreme intelligence of the divine light of consciousness. What I have seen many patients do at this stage is begin to relax and go very deep, but as body identification loosens its hold and they realize the material world and the person they thought they were is dissolving, they yank themselves back into the familiar world of the physical. It is very unsettling for them. Energy work helps them to settle into the bliss of the light of consciousness, which is God's love, and to rest there much longer. The infusion of sacred energy is very soothing, calming the actively dying on all levels. It is a great gift to receive this transmission of divine love during a time of life when one is most vulnerable.

* * *

Dad

One day I received a call that my dad had had a fall and was taken to the hospital where his head was scanned and it was found that he had a large blood clot in his brain. The decision was made to operate as the bleed was growing quickly. After the surgery, my dad could answer questions but he wasn't really waking up much — a nasogastric tube was placed for feedings due to his poor swallow. The surgeons still believed at this point that there was a good chance that he would recover, but after a few days this prognosis was proving to be wrong. A few days after his surgery I received a call that he was being prepped for a peg tube (which is a tube that is placed directly in the stomach to help him eat) so he could be moved to a nursing home. When I went to see my dad that day, he was showing obvious signs of actively dying. His eyes were rolling upwards, he was not alert and he was having long periods of apnea (periods where he was not breathing), along with secretions in his throat. I told the hospital staff to discontinue placing a peg tube as my dad was showing obvious signs of transitioning. The surgeon was not totally convinced at first and he said that there was nothing medically that should be causing his decline, but he agreed that my dad was looking worse everyday. Also, he was calling out in pain as every part of him hurt to be touched. The staff, fortunately after some discussion, came together quickly in agreement that my dad would go to comfort care only. The surgeon said, "We will see how he does with all the tubes out and if he is indeed moving towards passing away." It was agreed that a morphine drip would be started immediately, the nasogastric tube removed and all efforts would be made to keep him pain-free and breathing easily. Certainly if my dad's swallow returned and he became stronger then we would move in this direction, but at this point his body was obviously shutting down and it felt only right to work in harmony with this as the line towards the possibility of his recovery was crossed.

Later that day I went back to hospital and his room looked much calmer. He was still on the intensive care unit, but the staff had dimmed the lights and soft music was playing in the background. All his tubes were out and morphine was started. My dad continued to call out in pain and show progressive signs of actively dying. We talked about starting hospice, but the surgeon did not feel like there was a diagnosis that could be used and he still was not sure about the whole thing. Fortunately this made no difference as I was still able to get my dad all he needed for his comfort — and quickly. The morphine went up and up as he needed it — other medications were also given as needed for his comfort. The second day into comfort care, my dad had so much fluid in his lungs and throat that he sounded like he was drowning. Amazingly, at this point a nurse came in and said they wanted to move my dad to another floor as this was an ICU and they thought he would go quicker. The nurse said that his oxygen saturations were good and it looked like he was stable. I was very surprised by this statement and told him that the oxygen saturations and all the numbers on the screen made no difference — that my dad was showing prominent signs of actively dying and will pass away any minute… that in no way should he be moved. The nurse said he had twenty-four hours to stay on the unit and if he did not pass in that time, he would need to be moved.

    I sat in his room for a few more hours after this discussion listening to the rattly breathing, speaking softly to him and putting a cold cloth on his forehead. Then I went to take a break and get some fresh air. When I returned to my dad's room he looked very ashen, but his oxygen saturations were holding steady, his heartbeat and rhythm were also mostly steady — his pulse at this time was 80 beats per minute. The nurses were watching the monitor and one said, "Is there someone he is holding on to see?" I said, "There is no one he would be waiting for, but me." I then got another cool cloth for his head and placed one hand on his head and one on his heart. I said to him, "I love you dad. I am here — go home now and be at peace." What happened next was remarkable; the life force of my dad moved directly from his head to his heart, his breathing became completely still and quiet, then a few more quiet breaths with no rattle and then one more gasping breath… and then none. The screen the nurses were looking at went from full signs of life to flat line in five minutes time. The life force of my dad saturated the heart area and then a lightness was felt — floating and a gentle peace pervaded the room.

The hospital staff was amazed. The male nurse who was going to move him said, "Wow, it didn't look just a minute ago that he was going so quickly — then you just walked in and… he must have been waiting. I really believe that." I said, "He was waiting."

* * *

Blessings on your journey Dad.

Star light

Moon shine

Glory is this fine state

where wandering never ceases

and one is as open and fluid as

the river and space

One is so very weary

shut the eyes and see that the heavens

are made of you

the wind, the bird's call, the child's laugh

and tears are calling you home

My dear friend,

look out

all that is seen is your very

soul

wanting to get to know you

and see you smile

Light up the world

sweet and happy

the rushing ocean

the rising sun melting

and all the worries

have melted too

This joy

this beauty

love live laugh

Where did you come from?

the heavens

the earth

the holiest place

the night call

and sky

fly tonight

the moonrise is in the

background

and will light your way

the velvet night

will be your blanket

when you get tired

I am that child that giggled

so long ago

and looked at the color dancing

all around

dancing

whirling

always at play

what a beautiful rock

and a special bright flower

would you like to play?

Sing, sing

the ocean sounds in the heart

floating in this rhythm

what glory

what peace

so soft

light as a feather

and solid as the earth

this beingness

never dies

Love sweet

love

holy always

within beauty

stilled

and pure

Energy Work

Energy work:

- *Helps enhance the effectiveness of pain medications so patients can use less and remain clearer*
- *Helps relax the breathing, which brings further rest to the mind and soul*
- *Helps settle the mind and heart so one can merge into the new journey that awaits and rest in the arms of God's love*
- *Helps clear lifetimes of mental clinging and debris in consciousness*
- *Helps move the soul onto the new journey rather than remain stuck in the habitual mental drama of past lives*
- *Helps resolve internal conflict and regret*
- *Brings peace to the heart and mind and a sense of being loved and safe*

* * *

Steve

His hands rested on her forehead and heart, her breathing was smooth and moved through the being from head to toe, her eyes were semi-open and wore a serene gaze as if deeply internal. There was no strain or struggle to her features... and when this young man moved his hands, he looked tenderly at her — her breathing deepened in response to his attentive presence, her entire being soaking in the rays of healing. I watched from the doorway, as I did not want to interrupt the tender scene. The young man finally looked up and greeted me. He told me he was this woman's son and was only twenty years old. He had a graceful, light manner and smiled easily as we spoke.

His mother was young, in her early fifties — her diagnoses: glioblastoma (brain tumor). She was non-verbal and looked as if she had just days to survive. Her son, Steve, told me he had never studied or done healing work, yet he appeared to be a natural healer — the power of love easily guiding his hands, effortlessly soothing any traces of suffering in his mother... the connection between the two mutually nourishing. This is healing at its finest, flowing through a heart of simplicity that truly loves for love's sake and only wants to release and relieve — wanting nothing for itself, but only to bring happiness and in so doing there is no sense of being outside of this experience, but embraced within it — no division — only love moving.

* * *

"This makes me feel so good, I feel like getting up and dancing a jig." — *Quote from a 104-year-old patient, transitioning to actively dying while receiving energy work.*

Energy work, Reiki, healing touch and all other healing modalities literally mean *universal life force*. It is through the universal life force that healing takes place. When healing is transmitted from a point of still mind, the pure life force can do its inherent work of dissolving what needs to be dissolved, healing what needs to be healed, opening what needs to be opened and bringing to light what needs to be seen and released.

Universal energy, like spirit, does not conform to personal expectation and should not be reigned in by doership. The most potent healers were and are sages — the pure beings who rest in Christ-consciousness. Void of self-centered motives due to ego dissolution, there is a direct transmission that occurs in the presence of such beings. The holy ones that have entered the kingdom of heaven (moksha) while embodied do not utilize intention, manipulation, strategy, doership, guides, visualization or any technique. These holy ones have *become* the all healing universal force that emanates very powerful, drawing rays of silence capable of pulling one out of the mesmerizing spell of maya. This potent healing force has the capacity to loosen and dissolve the knot of attachment to mind and body, which in turn can alleviate concentration on bodily defects, bringing about a sense of being connected to something far greater than the physical.

To give food to one that is hungry is wonderful, to put a band-aid on a wound that is bleeding brings comfort, but to aid in the transformation of the individual to pure spirit brings everlasting bliss and freedom from the round of death, rebirth and suffering. Such is the workings of the sage (the embodiment of the pure universal life force).

There was a gentleman who said something to me when I was India. He said that he knew a woman that helped bring the spirit out of the body when someone was actively dying. I replied that the timing of death is not within our control and the response to transmission of universal energy towards the end of life varies greatly: some go quickly as if in a burst of flames, almost as if all leftover debris surfaces in a concentrated manner as fuel for pure spirit and *whoosh... this one is released from form*; others go amazingly slowly and may rest in the actively dying state for way beyond the usual process. The transmission of universal energy in this case grants them more time to complete whatever unfinished business is left in the psyche. Whatever takes place on the outside is not to be judged. The pure intelligence will move in, take over and what takes place is always for the greatest good.

Shifts occur within the system when a new agent (pure consciousness) is introduced and sooner or later subtle openings emerge, allowing the light that radiates from the core of being to pierce through... it is then that new insights and understandings come bringing a greater understanding of who one truly is...

There are some that appear to not respond to energy work in a manner that can be described. They are not able to verbalize shifts or movement. In spite of this, however, work is being done. When a transmission of energy is given, something new moves through the being at all levels and like a ray of warm light, the pure energy begins to soften that which is bound by matter. Like the seed that rests deep in the dark earth, the universal life force continues to penetrate the soil (whatever consistency the soil may be). There is work being done and that seed will be penetrated by this purifying force sooner or later, which will set the cycle of nature in motion. The seed deep in the earth rests outside of one's awareness and depending on the level of receptivity, the tender sprout will take time to break through into conscious awareness.

A sense of well-being and relaxation is

an immediate benefit of energy work.

Just as all fully enjoy a warm, spring day — the majority of recipients respond in a positive manner to transmission of universal energy. It feels good. Troubles recede. There is a greater sense of relaxation for no reason at all. It is effortless. It flows, it sings — it just *is*. There are some who upon receiving the very first treatment, open up like one thirsty for pure water. These recipients bloom and in the very moment, appear to reconnect at a deep level with past spiritual progress and set off from here to continue forward — a joy and wonder to witness.

* * *

Peter

Peter was a gentleman in his late fifties who had cancer that metastasized to the brain. His family was a loving, very close, social group who enjoyed crowding around his hospital bed at the nursing home — the family's two little dogs joining in as well. Peter had a very quiet, sweet, gentle demeanor, almost childlike and was very open to receiving energy work. Peter lived in a small town, sheltered from the rush of the city. He enjoyed listening to the "oldies but goodies" while receiving energy work, and, while the treatments were given, the family was right there chitchatting. The dogs could be heard munching on treats (the lights were on most of the time).

For a few of the sessions, I was able to work on Peter when the family was gone and would dim the lights — the quiet, darkened room helping him go deeper much quicker. Peter absorbed the energy well and would always be sleeping or in a deep meditative state during and after. What was very interesting about this case was that Peter remained in the actively dying state for over three weeks — a state which most pass through relatively quickly (one to five days is the norm). Upon leaving him, several times, he was exhibiting all the signs of a very ripe transition, which continued on for days and days. He did not appear uncomfortable. His friends and family said all the right things. They told him it was okay to let go. All was done to aid in his passing but he remained resting in this transitional state. When he did eventually pass, he did so quite comfortably and peacefully.

* * *

Universal healing needs no aim or intention. Being complete, whole (holy) in and of itself, this energy pulls what is whirling around on the periphery towards and into its perspective center, which is a natural, effortless movement of its pure guiding forces.

Lena and Michael

Michael was a middle-aged gentleman with a genetic disorder called genetic ataxia, which affected him in a systemic manner. Primary symptoms were poor balance and dementia. He came onto hospice after he was diagnosed with pancreatic cancer. Michael was a very dear, innocent presence, always smiling — a joy to be around. Lena, his wife, was very attentive to his physical needs, very present for him, even with the demands of work and caring for adult children (who also have this disorder).

From the beginning, Lena was exceptionally open to discussing spirituality as a means to healing, which created an extremely receptive atmosphere for spiritual discussion and energy work — something I do not come across often. The general feel of what flowed so easily through Lena's presence was an openness to working through the heart; an openness to moving with this process in a detached, loving manner, to being fully present and to embrace Michael's journey as a gift. When energy work (which Lena calls, "the blessing") was given to Lena she connected very deeply to an extremely rich spiritual life that was covered over for quite some time. Although she always had a very devotional heart, life experiences had moved her away from the true purpose of being alive. Lena soaked in the energy, like a dry garden that was waiting and watching for the first rains. She basked in blissful rays of peace and joy in the coming days and went deeper each time she received the universal energy. Michael drew in the energy easily, immediately went into a deep meditation and remained this way for quite some time. Often, when I left, he was still in this state.

The visits went on this way. Lena continuing to emanate a rare, devotional, loving, yet detached presence, basking in the joy of the unfolding moment and open to the blessing of Michael's process. Michael was quite calm and pain-free for some time. Then one day when I came over, Michael exhibited symptoms of what looked like hyperventilation. This was something he had displayed in the past, but not to this degree. He was alert at this time, smiling as usual, but breathing in this manner. I visited Michael on Friday and Michael passed away forty-eight hours later.

What came forward for Michael were some very sudden, intense symptoms: seizures, confusion and restlessness — which lasted for some hours into the night. The next day Michael died.

The hospice team and doctor that worked with Michael were shocked that this process was so rapid.[14]

Lena remained very open through Michael's entire journey, treating him with unconditional love and seeing all as a blessing, fully surrendered to the unfolding experience even though it did not turn out as planned. We discussed the blessing of Michael's final days being very quick so that he was spared a long, drawn out bed bound existence. Lena was and is a steady light of grace, unconditional love and devotion. This light seemed to glow even brighter with her beloved Michael's passing.

Below is a letter Lena wrote to friends and family after Michael's passing:

Dear friends,

We are at last back in our apartment after a very devastating windstorm. We are taken in by dear friends who made us feel so very welcome. We now have our power, heat and phone service back. It is still cold here but I am glad to be back and receive our mail and move forward with funeral plans. We have been receiving lovely cards, flowers and phone messages and are so grateful that you think of us at this time. I apologize for not sending out any Christmas cards. I will send a letter to each one of you after the holidays when I have time to make a personal love note for all kindness and prayers with the loss of our dear (Michael). A friend said to me that this Christmas

---

[14] Sometimes people pass in this manner, but it is not as common.

would be very sad because (Michael) would not be here but I can't agree... it is (Michael's) graciousness, innocence and joy that are the heart of the Christmas season. He was so happy with any kindness toward him that, despite the dark we were faced with during the storm, the light that shone within him illuminated our way.

Wishing you all peace, love and light,

—(Lena) and family

* * *

Healing work, a very ancient art, has unfortunately throughout the years become increasingly commercialized, which sometimes involves expensive crash courses or even more expensive long-term courses. Though it is convenient to have instruction available to the public in this way, it must be understood that this commercialized style of instruction loses something in the process. Traditionally, throughout time, healing work was passed down by an elder and never involved memorization, strategy or learned technique — it flowed spontaneously through transmission in relationship with a wise soul.[15]

---

[15] Understandably, a personal connection with an awakened master is not at hand for all, but if one is going to undertake healing work, it is important to appreciate that the pure life force is inherent and does not require traditional learning. This keeps the heart open to new possibilities and experiences that can, over time, help guide one to a teacher or master that works solely in a state of pure intuition.

Accumulated knowledge dampens the power, brilliance and purity of the universal life force.

Zero-Point Balance

It was through the relationship with Swami-G that healing work evolved for this Swami (Siddhananda). Never was one thing written down or memorized; there was never a class taken. One day when Swami-G was doing healing work, she told me she thought I would be good at it, and from there, we began working together.

The healing work founded by Swami-G is called *0-point*, which means while resting in meditative or still mind, the healing occurs. Swami-G and I used to do energy work at a local Indian teashop in Seattle and the feedback we received from the majority — if not all — was that the energy was far less scattered than other healing modalities, including Reiki. Most, after receiving the energy work said, "Whoa!" and had to sit for a while and reported they felt as if transported into another state of consciousness that most described as *expansive, very soothing, bliss-like and healing* — all good reports. One woman (who was a healer herself) said, "I told my friends, if you really want good healing done, come to the Kundalini healers."

When Kundalini bloomed in full years back, I was very ill with months of nausea, physical pain, insomnia as well as emotional and consciousness shifts that were frightening for me and left me ungrounded. All of these symptoms were made much worse because I had no understanding of what was occurring. I had never had healing work done or felt a desire to do so, but was so in need of balance that I went to a few healers that were recommended by friends. All the experiences exacerbated the symptoms, leaving me extremely dizzy, nauseous and with increased anxiety. None of the healers with whom I spoke could explain kundalini — including kundalini yoga instructors or any yoga instructors for that matter. Meeting Swami-G very quickly calmed these symptoms down and balance slowly returned, as well as a steady clearing of consciousness. When Swami-G did healing work on me (which was not until a few years after I met her), the experience was so different from what had been experienced with other healings. The main difference was the experience of expansiveness, peace, no-mind, bliss, internal rest; this experience carried over throughout the day. The whole experience was grace, completely balanced, completely harmonious, as if one was being moved to the center of being, not pulled and scattered outward.

When I started doing healing work with Swami-G, she told me that a still or meditative mind is the best protection,[16] no boundaries or clearing processes are needed before or after. It

---

[16] When the mind stills, energy is experienced as neutral, not colored by the attitude and judgment of the practitioner — stillness is what holds the mind and heart in a perpetual state of purity — a state in which influences of negative and positive karma cannot stick to it. A deep meditative state during healing does not come easily, but is the outcome of years of dedicated spiritual efforts as well as a steady connection with an illumined master. It can't be stressed enough that one should be under the guidance of a healer that works in a 0-point state (of which there are none that I know of except Swami-G and myself) before discontinuing clearing techniques. If the student is interested, it is wise to look for a teacher who talks about working from a state of pure intuition and appears to practice what is being preached.

was not until meeting Swami-G that I experienced the bliss of still mind and this easeful state continues intermittently to this day. What was noticed when doing healing work was that as soon as the hands made contact with the recipient, the mind would still automatically and that the work would take place in a completely effortless manner — the hands moving on their own in a fluid fashion, guided by the pure intuition of the divine force. The work is and remains a deep meditation in itself, an extremely holy experience that is not separate from spiritual practice, but a continuation of a steady, clearing, holy divine, substantial experience. I have also done a lot of self-healing as kundalini phenomena, pain, exhaustion and prolonged periods of illness have continued off and on. I have not been able to take any medications due to extreme sensitivities.[17] I have noticed that the self-healing sessions have made the healing work all the richer.[18]

The deep pool of pure intelligence is

what does the work of healing...

The feel of universal energy is like the feel of consciousness itself. When doing the work in still mind, the body does not feel solid... and when the eyes are closed, the hands

---

[17] The spiritual teachings and the relationship with Swami-G have brought more endurance to these periods of ailing health and consciousness has continued to clear as the physical condition has not affected spiritual progress in any way.

[18] Self-healing is primarily spontaneous and comes forward on its own. Self-healing does not need an agenda as it flows from the same source of pure intelligence and is much more effective when ego is put aside or dissolves.

resting on the body of the recipient, it feels as if dipping into a deep, dark pool of pure intelligence — which is exactly what is doing the work in a flow of pure, divine love.

Healing work and spiritual practice

Healing work is the result of deep spiritual cleansing and flows as a continuation of a heartfelt desire to be one with God. This is what makes the flow effortless, beautiful, bountiful, lasting and sustaining. It is when the divine force is allowed to move unrestrained that the recipient can come closer to the heartbeat of the universal soul and sooner or later experience in whatever manner the spark of the divine that is *who and what* they truly are — which is the greatest healing. When spiritual efforts are absent in the practitioner (which could simply be due to a misunderstanding or lack of exposure to the true heart of healing), then there is a very different outcome as the energy is funneled through a narrow field.

The results[19] felt by the recipient are either a scattered, diffused sensation or an extreme of a particular sensation that may result in some positive effects (shifts in the physical being or a sense of relaxation) as universal energy is working, working all the time (such is the giving way of the universe), however, the holiness of healing gets lost. It is a sincere heart of openness, a willingness to give up, an ability to let go that needs to be present in the practitioner for the most potent spiritual

---

[19] These effects are less likely to bring the recipient to a balanced state.

experiences to be transmitted because *silence and surrender* are the most drawing of all powers.

When the mind is still,[20] the energy is paused and contained with the very potent, inherent aim of pulling one into the heart and then the experience leaves the practitioner resting in still mind or God-consciousness unchanged, or the experience is mutually nourishing, mutually cleansing — an uninterrupted flow of heartfelt sadhana or spiritual practice. This is the *all healing* power of the universal life force. So it is best to leave *I am the healer* out of the whole equation, because when resting in still mind there is no *you* or *I*, there is just the palpable presence of the one healing power of God.

Pure and Impure Energy

Energy in and of itself is neutral. It is mind that colors judgment into it and the more one can settle into quiet mind, healing can be seen for the pure force that it is. When one is resting in a meditative mind, the divisive quality of mind that brings the feeling of, *I am healing someone that has such and such personality... such and such problems... such and such history*, dissolves. The divisive quality of mind that brings the feeling of otherness dissolves and there is just healing. Nothing

---

[20] If one finds that the mind wanders during healing work, come back to the breath. Treat the experience as holy and divine — treat the experience as sadhana. See it as an opportunity to progress. Give the fruits of the healing to God. In this way the seeds of surrender and renunciation will be nourished and healing will become rejuvenating and refreshing for all involved. With continued sincere practice, the mind will eventually quiet down little by little.

is felt as high or low, ugly or beautiful, pure or impure — these opposites are concepts of mind only and when nurtured internally, solidify positive and negative aspects of mind, which in turn takes the holiness out of healing and as a consequence there is a different result. One of the greatest healers of our time was/is Jesus and one can be assured he did not put boundaries around himself or spend time clearing. He did not remove himself from a particular disease or mindset of another — all were seen as one — and because of his divine, pure egoless presence, very powerful healing took place.

It should be understood that powerful healing does not necessarily mean one is immediately cured of a physical ailment.[21] Sometimes this happens, but this type of cure is completely secondary because if spirit is not nourished and brought forward, physical disease and ailments will continue to be reborn and replayed until consciousness can be cleared, the suffering mind dissolved and union entered. Some great sages passed through very serious illnesses (some died of cancer or were ill off and on throughout their lives), but through these physical shifts, consciousness continued to clear or remained pure, residing in God. Therefore it is not the form that is the priority; it is the eternal, everlasting spirit that, when brought into manifestation, moves one completely away from attachment to mind and form — this is everlasting healing. The form will

---

[21] Healing is not just of body... one is truly healed when the personal identity is merged for good in the ocean of universal consciousness. In this state, all suffering ceases — suffering being the feeling of a separate self.

continue to have its ailments — its aches and pains — but one knows through direct experience, that the form is a covering, only temporary housing — not the eternal — and so focus remains steadfast on and in God. Physical ailments can and do shift and oftentimes there are spontaneous healings at the hands of a saint. This is the beauty and miracle of the universal energy that is all loving, all powerful — all healing.

Intention of the Practitioner

I must acknowledge that I do not know in order to begin...

When one starts out on the spiritual path, it is because there is an intention to be free of suffering or to love and help others. As one moves forward and progresses, purposeful intention falls away, leaving the pure life stream with its inherent intention to love purely and to bring all to their highest good. Purposeful, loving, positive intention has value up to a certain point, but one must realize that loving intention comes from God — as all is given by God — and to hold intention is not necessary as it solidifies the sense of doership and being separate from the universe.

When I say I do not know, your knowing fills me completely — then beauty moves...

Holding intention can create problems for the recipient. Anything that is purposely held by the practitioner results in drawing the forces of mind into the healing, which is what gets transmitted to the patient. There may be positive results (hopefully), but there is far less hope of bringing the recipient to a higher level of consciousness. This is because when the self-centered movement of mind is part of the mix, the forces at play are more divisive, less concentrated — like the scattered, diffuse rays of a light bulb compared to a laser. The laser is the still mind, penetrating, deep, pure — this is the power of God's love — which will produce a very different result for the recipient. Also, resting in meditative mind will be nourishing and healing for the practitioner as well. So for both parties, bringing a quiet mind to healing, free from personal intention, is optimal.

A heart of innocence is what teaches us we are one...

The more one relaxes into the present moment, the smoother the pure life force can flow and do the work. In a state of attentive relaxation, all that is needed for healing comes forward in an effortless way. The practice of being present and letting go of doership removes the burden of feeling the need to *do* something — that it is our responsibility to do all good things on our own, that it is our responsibility to make a change.[22] The

---

[22] Letting go of intention does not mean one becomes irresponsible, but rather gives up attempts to control the outcome of the healing.

feeling of being personally responsible is very burdensome (even if it feels it is for the good). God never gave us this burden to carry and one is invited to lay it down and trust that the *one heart* will take care of all.

Let the healing love you...

To bring to healing the thought, "I am going to put my love into this suffering person," is a very subtle, play of ego, separating the soul of the practitioner from the one in need. We are all of one soul, one heart and *love is one* — there is no need to manufacture a recipe for healing. It is all right there at hand and comes so easily when mind gives up doership/personal responsibility and settles into the deep silence of the moment. A more open attitude brought to the healing is to let the healing love *you*.

Kundalini and Healing

It is very dangerous for a healer to intentionally attempt to open Kundalini in a recipient or to encourage practices towards this aim. Channels can be opened prematurely that can potentially bring very serious imbalance, which can fuel emotional disturbances, consciousness shifts, bodily pain, pressure and movement (kriyas), trembling, delirium, psychoses and distrust. Kundalini will open when it is time and it is not in our hands to push or force this potentially very volatile, potent energy. This energy is to be honored and left alone to Mother Nature's timing. If Kundalini is awakened in a recipient and the practitioner is not knowledgeable or dedicated towards selflessness and does not have a balanced spiritual practice in place, to continue to work on one with an awakened kundalini is doing a great disservice to the recipient. The energy work should be stopped and the recipient given grounding exercises, such as meditative walking, light meditation and gentle stretching. Also, the recipient should be directed towards one that is an authority in this matter. It is important as a healer to know when you have gotten yourself in too deep and to redirect the patient towards one who can help.

When one has a strong spiritual foundation in place as well as a competent spiritual guide, Kundalini will awaken on its own time. The manifestation of this divine energy will be much more balanced, gentle and the beneficial results be felt sooner. Zero-point energy work is very effective on clients with an awakened Kundalini. It calms the phenomena[23] and speeds up consciousness clearing or it may rev up phenomena in a balanced manner so that consciousness clearing takes place smoothly.

---

[23] Phenomena: anything that can be perceived or observed. Any state or process known through the senses, rather than by intuition or reasoning. Some of the classic phenomena related to kundalini are seeing lights and visions, ringing in the ears, movements and pressure on the limbs and consciousness shifts. For further explanation of kundalini, the reader is referred to Swami-G's book, "Kundalini from Hell to Heaven."

Reiki

The Japanese translation of "reiki" is "spiritual" or "sacred energy."

Reiki is a transmission of universal energy that flows from pure intuition and evolves out of years of dedicated spiritual practice.

The Reiki hands-on healing/spiritual practices were founded by Mikao Usui (a Buddhist monk) in early twentieth century Japan. After Mikao Usui immersed himself for years in deep spiritual practices, such as meditation, prayer and surrender, this healing came spontaneously and was based completely on pure intuition. The students who were interested in learning Reiki needed to adhere to very disciplined spiritual practices before moving onto the next level. The West has taken Reiki and made it almost exclusively an energy healing system of which spirituality is not a requirement. This has done a great disservice to humanity. The crash courses offered in the West cannot do justice to the ancient wisdom of Reiki. The students that take these courses are very ill-equipped to begin healing work in the community, as time has not been taken to help lay a steady spiritual foundation, which is the base from which all healing flows. That we all have within us ancient healing knowledge is without a doubt true, but to uncover this great jewel takes time, dedication and proper mentoring, which unfortunately these quick courses cannot offer.

Symbolism and Healing

Today, the practitioners of Reiki utilize symbols for healing that are transmitted through attunements by a Reiki master. These symbols are to be held in consciousness by the practitioner while doing healing work.[24] The symbol system's original use was not for healing, but symbolic of the spiritual path to enlightenment. Each symbol is representative of the levels of awareness that are passed through as one evolves in spirit and eventually enters union with the divine (enlightenment). A Reiki master is meant to be one who has completed the spiritual journey and rests in still mind and then healing manifests as a by-product to this pure level of consciousness. I find it very interesting that students memorize these symbols, call them up and hold them in consciousness while doing healing work because the symbols are only representations of levels of evolving consciousness, which takes direct experience to know.[25] When mystical experiences open, which bring direct experience with the divine, all symbolism falls away — just like worship of deities can take one only so

---

[24] Swami-G told me about the symbology used in Reiki quite awhile after I had been doing healing work. I had never read or heard about these techniques before.

[25] Spiritual symbology has come from and through the Rishis, the yogis, the monks or the far seers that through divine union, God has spoken and these symbols spontaneously emerged like the yantra, the mantra — all the holy imagery. Spiritual symbology is not meant to be memorized or strained over, but enjoyed, meditated on and relaxed into so that the ancient vibratory energy the symbol represents can help break up mental clinging.

far. If these symbols are perpetually taken to be something that is external or something that has power in itself, one will never go beyond into realization that these symbols are pointing to what rests within them and therefore the opportunity to progress beyond dual consciousness into eternal consciousness will, for the moment, be lost.

I have come looking

for I have lost my way

now where will you turn me

in what direction

for my heart is asking

though the words may not

be coming through clearly

teach me

the way

of love...

Healing work is truly meant to be a path to enlightenment, not meant as a system of gathering, collecting more tools, more strategies, more this and that. When one holds anything in mind,[26] be it symbols, intention, etc., there may very well be a potent transmission of energy, but the results are riskier, skewed, scattered or confused because the symbol is only as pure as the heart that holds it and when the heart is completely purified, the symbol falls away and is never thought of or needed again. The divine force has become the center, which is far more majestic, graceful, all healing and all loving than anything seen by the eye or memorized by the mind. When the mind falls silent, fully awake and receptive, Reiki is there in its purity, healing is there in its purity and no other exists.

Healing is not dependent on a 'you' or a 'me.'

Calling Up Internal Guides in Healing Work

That help is given from the other side is without question and all one needs to do is rest in this faith — when this faith becomes a living reality, the need to call up guides because something internal feels lacking falls away. What remains is pure intelligence that does not rely on imagination or any other. This intelligence (which is what you are minus the projections of mind) does the work of healing, which is a much more reliable, steady, peaceful way of being.

---

[26] Holding symbology in mind maintains the feeling of otherness (dual consciousness), which for the time being disallows the opportunity to melt away the sense of being separate from the universe.

When internal guides are encouraged in the psyche, it becomes difficult to discern what is of ego because the message of the internal guide becomes twisted so easily by one's conditioned impressions, and many times, guides are just constructs of one's imagination, saying what one wants to hear, confirming the ego, confirming the personal view. Anything else that is brought into the view is filtered through this imaginative internal guide to serve the personality and to keep one under the illusion of ego safety.

Releasing the shields

to the heart

opening to the light

that abides there

A song that reaches

farther than what I

can grasp

All that is not me

has fallen

and you have embraced me

with the understanding...

The healer and the healed

are one

To encourage the student to rely on internal guides is very risky because one who is drawn to this practice is often somewhat lost themselves and not yet able to accept or open up to the more intense paths that aid in removing the coverings to the universal soul. The discriminative powers of mind are usually quite weak in one who is drawn to internal guides. This one cannot discern what is of pure intent from the darker forces of the psyche and can very well, through ignorance and following the herd or following the instructions of the teacher, be thrown way off balance into a vivid world of imagination.

When one calls on guides, other forces in the psyche follow, which continues the cyclic movement of the seasons of mind: depression, clinging, etc. When this mindset is brought to healing, the results can be disastrous for the energy is very ungrounded.

To encourage guides does the student a great disservice for it adds more complications and clutter internally, weakening the mind and discriminative faculties and leading to confusion and a sense of being scattered — it further roots the sense of dual consciousness, which brings one farther away from the possibility of experiencing the true being which is of one nature. The clinging to guides may arise from fear of aloneness — to encourage this practice pushes away the possibility of seeing through this great illusive fear so that one loses for the time, the chance to move to a more vibrant, higher level of consciousness — a level where there is a sense of being connected to the whole.

God's light is what makes healing possible...

Silence is Master

One does not have to make a huge impact while doing healing, but simply stay steady, immersed in silence. Silence is the most potent attunement, as it will bring the student's scattered mind to center. This is the greatest healing. In this silence, all of the potent energies of the great masters of healing are poised and concentrated and at the ready to be of the highest service.

Imbalance in the Practitioner

> *Me reflecting more me*
>
> *a prism of desire*
>
> *I lay it down*
>
> *beside the heat of your love*
>
> *by your warmth*
>
> *I am renewed*

If the practitioner is depressed, physically ill, mentally scattered and confused, taking drugs, alcohol or void of dedicated efforts towards spirit, healing work should be stopped and time taken out for meditation and prayer, fresh air given to the spirit — renewed life to the soul. When one feels refreshed and steady, healing may be started again (with continued spiritual practices in place). One may be surprised at how different the healing feels after some time put forth for spiritual renewal.

To take time out when there is imbalance is to be responsible to yourself and your clients.

You (pure love) will never let me fall...

Can Universal Energy Do Harm?

Though I don't seek to hurt

I don't yet understand

Please teach me how to love.

When mind enters into the equation of healing, there is a very different result and the truth is that purposeful strategy, intentional manipulation of energy and intentional manipulation of the psyche can indeed cause harm. There have been many recipients of Reiki and other energy/healing modalities that have come to Swami-G and expressed that they feel much worse after receiving a healing. Sometimes the energy opens up channels of which the recipient is unprepared to manage or kundalini is opened or the symptoms exacerbated, which leaves the recipient more ungrounded, confused and uncertain where to turn. It has been made evident through experience that Reiki practitioners and yoga instructors appear to know very little about how to help navigate one safely through the kundalini process — having no direct experience with it themselves. Also, the instructors are not available for the student at all times when there are questions or challenges. The time with the student is limited to the very brief sessions and then the recipient is left to his/her own devices.

It is a very responsible role to be a healer or a teacher; to honor this role is to work in a manner that leaves the recipient increasingly refreshed and able to move forward with a lighter spirit and greater clarity. If one is truly interested in healing others, then to begin to look within yourself is the first step. To be open to leaving ego out of the equation of healing is a very important beginning. To develop a spiritual practice or work with a teacher who is dedicated to the aim of internal peace is imperative if one truly desires to be of aid to others.

The words love speaks are come, come, come...

Universal Energy

Universal energy in itself is healing and nothing but this, nothing else added or taken away. Universal energy is neutral, pure like the clearest glass of water that can do nothing but soothe the parched soul, always nourishing and aiding in bringing new life to the garden of the heart. It can never be anything other than purifying, for this energy is the matrix of all of life. It *is* life.

> *Mind is the smoke from the fire*
>
> *I cannot see clear*
>
> *when I sit so far away from the glow*

Mind, however, darkens this energy, twists it, changes its course because, like the clear glass of water, consciousness will shape itself into or reflect the contents of its holdings. So then there is a different expression of energy when this divine power is manipulated by mind. This is why the sages speak of silence because only in the intelligent depths of silence and surrender will this universal energy be justly honored and given full play which will in turn do the highest good for humankind.

Intuition, Healing and the Divine Mother

Intuition: the immediate perception of truths independent of any reasoning process, instinctive knowledge. Intelligence that is inborn — intelligence that exists prior to experience.

Intuition shines through the mental processes and guides all souls through the waters of experience. Some are more attuned to the intuitive aspect of the soul and commune with it easily, following its intelligent guidance and therefore living a much richer, more sensitive existence. Intuition is not different than universal energy — they are one — and like universal energy, when mind is added, the mixture gets muddied. Intuition is likened to the wild animal, living instinctively, watching, waiting, moving away from danger swiftly and spontaneously, and setting down instinctively to rest where there is safety, good nutrition and all the abundant, natural resources of nature. This innate knowing is still yet fluid, moving from place to place in union with the divine forces of the universe.

Intuition in its purest form is no-mind as it functions perfectly and at its highest when manipulation, analysis and reasoning are absent. Intuition is not something one can learn, but one needs to become attuned to its pure, inherent light, settle into and eventually merge with it. At this point the mind becomes quiet and what remains is only divine intuition, which moves of its own pure knowing nature, always keeping one safe within itself and moving to ensure safety and the highest good for others. To uncover intuition, one needs to stay still and highly alert, like the wild animal, and at the same time let go of fear. Have trust and faith that the right situation will present itself for the greatest protection and greatest good. To be alert is to let go of personal expectations and observe in awe the great unfolding that presents itself from moment to moment. Synchronicity will become more evident, which is an example of how all of life is connected, one in spirit and moving to the same song of the heart.

To bring a sensitive, alert mind to healing is a priority. Be watchful and trusting of the great guide (the divine mother of the universe). It is she who will guide the hands, heart and mind through healing. She knows exactly what to do and when, so there is no need to worry or to try to heal another on one's own. Stay quiet and tune in to her direction. All grace, all healing, all love, she is, and she resides within you. Like a child who looks to the mother for direction — look to her. Allow her to guide you. Be still. Have faith. Be quiet. She is there. She is one with you, not separate... and so to nourish ego is to move apart from her all knowing spirit. Stillness and surrender are like the open door that welcomes this eternal movement of mother divine. She will never fail to come to your aid when the heart is open, innocent, welcoming and embracing.

The Recipient

The practitioner can aid the recipient by first and foremost being an example of one who is either fully immersed in the bliss of God-union or fully dedicated toward this aim. Being an example is truly at the core of healing as the energy flows effortlessly from this center of dedicated spirit. If the practitioner is not devoted sincerely towards spirit, this lack will eventually show up somewhere and there will be a price paid, which equals a drain on the practitioner, the recipient or both.

To do the recipients the highest service is to speak to them about following the breath, relaxing and staying in the moment. One can listen compassionately to the personal history, but there is no need to reinforce or encourage mental drama. To encourage simplicity and unity is of the highest and this can only be offered when healers are working on this themselves. It is very important to help the recipients stand on their own two feet, not to enable in any way shape or form — to be compassionate but lovingly detached.

To help move the ones who have offered themselves to your care towards simplicity and their own instinctive knowing is of the highest counsel.

It is always good to offer an exercise in between sessions to help one settle the mind so the universal energy can be absorbed easier. In the first session, the recipient has the defenses up, there is uncertainty, lack of trust — which is quite common — but as one continues on and the coverings begin to fall away, the mind and body become less resistive. To encourage the recipient to follow the breath when the mind becomes active is very important and to spend time in meditation in between sessions is also important. It is good if the healer can be open to an e-mail or call in between sessions if there are problems and it is my suggestion that this be free of charge — given from the heart as Seva (giving back to the universe).

Universal healing moves according to its own law — always with the same inherent purpose, regardless of how it plays out on the exterior — clearing, purifying, integrating, gathering one into the heart, bringing one closer to home, the heart, the soul or seed, the beauty, the true purpose — eternally working this way and, all the while, releasing… releasing... releasing…

Healing and the Layers of Mind

Mind accumulates in layers, which means there is a vast amount of the personality that rests out of one's conscious awareness. Mundane consciousness is the more surface layer of mind in which most dwell, totally unconscious that there are deeper structures underneath composed of a history of collected conditionings that influence mood and drive behavior. It is when this surface layer is jostled, thinned or disrupted that the deeper aspects of the personality are brought to light. When there is no anchor of faith or spiritual foundation in place, one very often runs quickly back to the surface when there is a crack in the self-created concepts of who one thinks he/she is.

Healing is a process

Healing light

meets the shore of mind

washing up like waves

churning all thought of division

to sand

and with each breath

the waves pull

into itself

my little life

dissolving

emerging

becoming

one

Though energy work is an aid to relaxation and well-being, there are periods during the process (as the layers of mind are thinned) that the deeper samskaras[27] are revealed — as a consequence there can be all sorts of releases — emotions, physical shifts, memories and thoughts can rush through as the pure life stream pushes up against the debris. It is important to let the recipient know that these shifts are quite common and not to be concerned about them.

The mental patterns and physical shifts revealed in relationship to receiving transmission of pure consciousness is not what matters; it is the degree of surrender and willingness of the recipient to let go of the emerging phenomena that determines healing.

---

[27] Samskaras are mental colorings from the past carried forward into the present.

Energy work is a catalyst for healing and can help the recipient experience a state of surrender, but like all gifts of the universe, the life force cannot make contact with a heart and mind that are determined to be resistive… and sometimes when the surface persona, the persona that one has become accustomed to, is challenged, there is a great threat. When one perceives that the superficial persona cannot be maintained and resistance[28] is encountered, there is a potential for harmful patterns to emerge such as mood swings, projections, paranoia, justification, fear, wallowing, depression and passive aggression. If these symptoms emerge, the recipient should be advised to stop energy work and to spend time in meditation to allow for distance on the mental drama as well as settling.

It is helpful to inform the recipient that healing is a process and there can be symptoms that manifest along the way that may not feel positive, but this does not indicate healing is not taking place. These shifts are transient and should not be labeled as a digression, but can many times indicate progress as the former seemingly solidified personality is beginning to wear down revealing a deeper layer of the self and in turn creating more internal space allowing for more light to enter as well as moving one closer to the core of being.

It is also helpful to discuss with the recipient the importance of staying in witness state, to not attach to the emerging content, to not put a spin of *me and my story* into it.

---

[28] Resistance can be purposeful or rest out of one's awareness, in either case, it is the willingness or ability to surrender that determines progress.

Many times, a recipient will comment that during energy work, though he/she was crying, there was no sadness felt. The recipient may have felt surprised at the emotion that came forward as if *out of the blue* and will express that there was no personal attachment to the experience. There was only stillness, a witness... a release and relief. If the recipient twists the release taking place and washes the personal history over it, then that is when harmful expressions can manifest. The healer can point out the misunderstanding and guide the recipient to stay with the breath — to reinforce that what is occurring is a transient happening — a good thing, no matter how it is playing out and to attach to the occurrence will only cause it to be held onto and repeated.

> *The healer cannot give to another that which has not been understood by direct experience.*
>
> *Be still and healing manifests.*
>
> *Healing is stillness in action.*

Energy Work, Physical Pain and the Elderly

The elderly are just like babies when receiving energy work; they sink into it with such trust and, almost without fail, are left sleeping like babies at the end of the session (oftentimes snoring).²⁹ The beauty of working with the elderly, especially in nursing homes, is that just a little initial chitchat needs to take place, a consent for energy work, and that is all. Very little information is needed. One does not need to know the religious preference, the family history, the internal drama — this is the beauty of universal energy, that it cuts through all that is separating, it is not dependent on personal history, religious preferences, age, education or anything external, displaying the intuitive beauty and unity of the universe that does not discriminate in even the slightest way. All beings are made of this energy and all are entitled to it — this is the universal song of silence that eternally pours forth its healing love.

Elderly patients know very little to nothing about energy work. The patients confined to nursing homes are debilitated, many confused and disoriented, yet these patients are truly my favorite to work on. There are no preconceived notions about the work, no expectations and therefore the energy is soaked in immediately in a pure manner. I would love to see this work make its way into nursing facilities as the healing touch is so desperately needed and appreciated there. When an elderly patient that has been suffering is left sleeping peacefully, this is the best thank you one can receive.

* * *

---

[29] I have found this to be true of teenagers as well, they soak in the energy like babies (probably due to not yet accumulating all the intellectual baggage) and though normally may be restless and hyper are left sleeping like babies, the body completely still for hours.

Camille

Camille was a patient on hospice in her late nineties. She had a diagnosis of Debility Unspecified, which means there was no primary disease process that brought her onto hospice, but rather a collection of symptoms and health problems that were causing her decline. When I walked into the nursing home to meet her, the family was gathered around her bed looking concerned. They told me she kept saying, "I want to die; I just want to go." Statements such as these are very common, especially with the elderly as they become so very weary of a bed-bound existence and are more than ready to move on to a new journey. Of course listening to these statements every few minutes was unsettling for the family.

When I met Camille, it was apparent she was in a lot of pain. She was grimacing and holding herself very tense, yet attempting to be social. She would greet you with a smile and then say, "Could you please help me die?" She continued to interject this question every few sentences. I told her we were not here to help her die, which would happen soon enough, but we could help make her much more comfortable so that the process would be more tolerable. The family was reluctant to give her pain medications because they wanted her to remain alert; they wanted to enjoy her company for as long as they could. Camille was very open to receiving energy work, which she absorbed immediately, and the best thing was that not more than five minutes into the energy work, Camille stopped asking everyone in the room to help her die. The family commented that they had not seen her this relaxed in a long while. Camille looked quite peaceful through the session, a distant soft gaze to her eyes. I discussed with the family the need for consistent pain management — that if Camille's pain were lessened, she could enjoy the rest of her days much more peacefully. The family finally agreed, seeing how Camille's presence shifted so quickly with the healing work.

It took quite some time to get the pain medications from the pharmacy, but I was able to work on Camille part of the time while we waited for them to arrive — this kept her peaceful. Camille was finally given some morphine, which acts very quickly (within ten minutes), and once this medicine took effect, Camille continued relaxed and did not beg again to help her die. I heard later that Camille lived several weeks longer, quite comfortably. She even played cards with her family and was a blessing to be around as her attitude was so warm and positive. There was never another mention of her asking to be helped to die again.

* * *

Violet

Violet was a very upbeat, elderly patient with a gracious manner about her. When I walked into Violet's room in the nursing facility, she was sitting on the edge of the bed so hunched over that her eyes were directed downwards at her feet. We got acquainted for a bit and during the conversation, she expressed chronic pain that was always present in her back and shoulders, which was not a surprise considering the position of her back and spine. We were never able to make eye contact due to the position of her body, but in spite of this, she was very intuitive, very sharp with a quick wit. She said it was fine to do energy work and after a while into it, she said, "Whatever you are doing, it feels so good." Not long into the session, she began to snore very loudly. Her muscles felt much more relaxed. After a while, I collected my bag quietly and left her to rest. I could still hear her snoring as I walked down the hallway.

* * *

Pain

Emotions such as fear, grief and despair can get locked into the cellular matter, organs and muscle, which can translate into disease and/or pain. When Kundalini first awakened years ago, it moved through the physical body encountering blockages and the results were full blown body pain.[30] My initial reaction was shock and then helplessness as I had never experienced pain to that degree and had no clue how to live with it or manage it. Pain medicines made all the symptoms worse. One night, I began massaging my legs and had an urge to allow the body to tell its story — to release whatever was being held there. What came through and continued to come through for a few years was a flood of emotion, long held sorrow and grief. It was a very long process of working with the body, of allowing, of waiting and

---

[30] It is advised to seek the advice of medical professionals and rule out any organic cause to physical symptoms.

watching, of enduring and at this time, I did not have a teacher, so I was going by intuition as well as the spiritual practices I had laid out for myself.

I needed to take time off work due to the symptoms and I continued to live daily in this way. Slowly, over the course of some months, the muscles became freed up and pain to that degree has never returned. As pain began to lessen, the helplessness and despair thinned out as well and there was some understanding of the universal love and healing that was ever present as it was experienced that this healing was not the result of an individual, but of a universal cleansing process. It is very important to have support if one is going through something like this. A connection to a competent spiritual mentor can help calm these emotions and bring one to balance much sooner.

Pain (and disease) can be a portal to higher consciousness. The more the mentation locks into pain, the greater the mind/body connection becomes, which in turn encourages more tension, decreased circulation, anxiety, shallow breathing and pain. Energy work can help to loosen the knots that keep the consciousness connected to physical symptoms and when these knots are loosened, the potential is present to enter a new dimension that is quite freeing.

Just as one is encouraged to not run away from emotion, shifting mental states and internal pain, it is also encouraged to not run from physical symptoms such as pain and disease. These symptoms have a story to tell and if one can sit with the body silently, patiently, attentively in a detached, loving manner, consciousness (the light of awareness) will begin to settle into these bound places and releases begin to take place. When there is pain, one can sit and place the hand there, breathe into the area, relax and begin meditation — awareness will go to that place and begin to illuminate what is held there.

It is very important to keep any emotions, imagery or clues to the personal history fluid — let them run through the open mind like a stream without clinging to them giving these phenomena a chance to be flushed. Placing a hand where there is holding in the body is a way to connect with it — almost like giving permission to allow Mother Nature to come and begin the cleansing. Do this activity with an open loving heart — one that is forgiving. If there is disease this same thing can be done. Breathe easily into the area — one will notice eventually a throbbing or pulsating under the hand as circulation and life are brought to the area. Healers do this quite naturally, but one can sit and do this on their own as well.

***

Annie

Annie was an elderly woman that I met through another friend that was receiving healing work. Annie was carrying some very heavy grief due to the recent loss of her son and a history of losses. In spite of this, she was very pleasant, open and friendly. She openly shared of her traditional Christian background and church community that brought her much comfort and support. She complained of pain in her right shoulder and said she knew nothing about energy work, but consented to it. She decided to sit in a chair while receiving the energy, which she absorbed quite readily. When I began working on her right shoulder, her head bent down and her body leaned back and melted into the chair and then she fell into a deep sleep, which was certain because later she began snoring. We all sat in meditation around her for some time and eventually she came to. She stood up looking so refreshed that she appeared fifty years younger. All who were present commented on her youthful appearance and we were laughing because it was wonderful to see her stand up smiling, looking like a brand new woman with a completely different energy about her. She said, "I have never had that happen before. Did everyone fall asleep?"

* * *

Testimonies

A report from a family member

(Michael) is quite serene and calm and still. We have been blessed by meeting a Swami who is also our hospice nurse. She has initiated[31] us both into the divine and I feel plunged into the sea of infinite bliss. (Michael's) death is no longer seen as an enemy but a harbinger of divine joy to be shared with all.

A letter written after doing healing work for a family

What a gift from the universe to have you grace our home yesterday. I wondered what to get for my mother-in-law and sister-in-law and YOU were it! To see the visible signs of eternal youth on my mother-in-law's face, the peace descend on my sister-in-law, was truly humbling. Thank you for being in divine communion and being the light bearer... I couldn't feel any closer to joy than now. All my e-mails have reflected the luster of your soul and if there has been light you are far nearer the source and that is grace. I know you will read behind and within the words and feel my heart in your own beat.

---

[31] Initiated — referring to energy work

Letter after healing work done at the ashram

Before coming to the ashram and taking diksha, my past practice was Vipassana meditation. With this method I found I was able to bring pain/blocks into awareness and watch the energy dissipate. However to reach the awareness necessary to dissolve the pain would require four to five days of sitting, cross-legged on the floor for up to fourteen hours a day. Even then, this could only take things so far as the deeper the blocks went, the deeper into stillness I needed to go in order to once again continue the clearing process. With the energy work, all that is needed is to lie down and relax! Swami-G works from 0-point balance. It seems that by surrendering to that stillness in which she is settled, which would literally take months (maybe years!) to clear through intensive vipassana meditation, is dissolved in that one session.

Report from a hospice social worker

Receiving energy work has been a deeply relaxing and profound experience. With a gifted and experienced practitioner, there is a definite transmission that takes place. During energy work, I feel a connection to the divine force — a molecular shift that is very peaceful and reassuring. I realize just how much I am not my body (which is one reason why this work can be so powerful with the dying who are preparing to transition out of their physical form).

For me, experiencing this brings home the power of this discipline and way of life — a path based on what may be the last remaining ancient religion based on an elemental connection and communion with the Universe.

The mind stills for a long while after the energy work session is complete. I sleep more deeply and remember dreams more vividly. If I'm having physical problems, the session usually works it through. I feel more present and able to transmit some of this calm to others, which is especially helpful for the hospice patients I work with.

Report illustrating benefits of regular energy sessions

When I first started energy work, I did not experience much but a bit of relaxation. This was due to the fact that I was ignorant of how to accept the gift that I had been offered.

In conjunction with energy work, I began dabbling in the practice of yoga and meditation. My heart, soul and body began awakening from a deep sleep and I was opened up to experiences and realizations I never knew existed.

My energy sessions begin with some deep relaxing breaths, allowing the belly to soften and letting go of the preoccupations accumulated throughout the week. My breath falls into a slow natural pattern and I try to still my mind. Intermittently and without effort, my lungs will completely fill from the abdomen and will release deeply. I feel my normally constricted left bronchial tube open up allowing air to flow. I usually have physical releases, which include eyes fluttering and upper body shuddering slightly from the head down through the neck, shoulders, arms and fingers. Occasionally, I will have an emotional release, which consists of a quick crying spell that seems to surface without any reason. All of these releases rid me of stagnation and allow fresh energy to flow freely throughout.

As a woman who has been battling cancer for many years and who shied away from all things spiritual, my weekly sessions play a major role in my newfound physical and spiritual health. My breathing has improved tremendously. I can't remember when I could breathe as freely and deeply as I do now. My overall posture and shoulder flexibility is better than it has been in years and most importantly, I feel healthy and well balanced in more ways than one.

At the end of the week, I yearn for the energy work. I now accept the gift fully and relish the experience.

Report from a student with active kundalini

For me, energy work is nothing short of a miracle that takes place in and around the body. It's the physical manifestation of the universe at the fingertips of the practitioner and patient. Receiving and giving energy work has been a transformative experience for me. At first, it was about lying still while the practitioner moved hands around your body. But it is much more than a massage.

Energy work helps balance out energy that is inherent and a part of your body. Sometimes, you can even feel the shifts taking place, whether it is a cramp that loosens or a clench of muscles that relaxes. In certain parts of the body, it can help activate or enliven chakras. For example, the practitioner may tap at my third eye — the area between my eyes — to open up intuition.

I have learned that energy work is also about meditation and breath. As a patient or healer, the idea is to empty the mind and focus on the breath coming out of your nose or in the stomach. The breath is not forced, but natural. Now, I am able to observe my natural breath throughout the day, which releases some tensions and stress. I even have a bit of a stomach pooch that shows how I have been tightening the muscles in the area without thinking — an area that holds a lot of stress and old identities.

Sometimes energy work will leave me completely relaxed and in the moment for the remainder of the day, or even the week. Sometimes it helps emotional release cycle through faster — so that you may not necessarily feel "great" but you know it is helping clear away old muscle memory.

Energy work is also about opening the heart to the healer, and connecting with their breath and their energy.

Now that I have had regular energy work — that is, once at least every two weeks — I definitely feel a difference. I am much more balanced than before, energy flows better (which helps lessen strong kriyas), and the path and practice towards realization becomes more of a daily part of my life.

One student put it this way:

"Energy work is not like a step, it is a leap *forward!"*

Chapter 5

Tools and Practices

This section offers tools and practices that help still the mind and open the heart to the divine light and wisdom inherent in the universe. These pointings are offered as daily practices that can be used at any and every given moment.

Follow the breath

Come back to the breath when one gets caught up in the mental world, pay attention to the movement of the breath in and out of the nostrils. The breath is like an anchor for a mind that runs out of control. Following the breath is one of the first practices given and is to be used again and again throughout the process.

A mindful day

Take a full day or a chunk of time out of the day to be fully aware and present to the flow of experience. When you are washing dishes feel the warmth of the water on the hands. When one is walking, know one is walking. When one is sitting, be aware that one is sitting. Is the seat hard or soft? Are the feet bare? Is the floor cold? Pay attention to the warm air coming in and out of the nostrils. Become aware of the easy rise and fall of the chest. Is one in a small or large room? If one finds there is nothing in particular to do — just sit. When the mind wants to go out into so many things — bills, kids, things that need to be done — just notice it. Gently bring the awareness back to the breath.

Is it very difficult to sit with no purpose?

It is good to take full days out to be mindful. Of course it is always nice to be alone, but one can be mindful in the midst of activity as well.

Feel your way

Take some time out of the day and live as one who has lost the physical vision. One does not have to be blindfolded for this activity but can wear a blindfold if that feels right. When moving about — feel your way. Relax as much as possible into intuitive awareness. Notice the degree of trust or lack of trust present, just notice it. Become aware of the texture of life, the feel of it. Is there a spaciousness about existence? When one is aware, does it feel divided or fluid? What is the mindset when one is moving about? Is it rushed or relaxed? Is there an urge to move onto the next thing? How does water *feel* on the hands?

How does the hug of child *feel* when held close to the breast? What does the smile of another *feel* like when connected with? To feel is to be fully intuitive, not relying on judgments, expectations or mental colorings. To feel is to be like an artist, a poet, a musician and to allow this presence to bloom and dance into every moment of existence. To *feel* your way is a very good exercise for healers and those who are interested in healing work. It heightens awareness of raw sensations as well as intuitive guidance. So, feel your way!

Go through the common

As we look at the body, our lives, our experiences and our children, the commonalities are so evident.

As the mind slows down through following the breath and spiritual practices, the commonalities of human experience reveal themselves quite easily. Insights will come that bring to light the unity of life. These insights are like flashes that show one there is another reality beyond the seemingly continuous mundane existence. To nourish a united vision within is to pay attention to the common experience that is present in the one experience.

It is by going through the common that the lonely, isolating, personal world of pain begins to thaw out. The mind works very hard at telling one that they are separate, but as internal clarity deepens, these myths of separation that we once took to be real and solid begin to look silly and it becomes increasingly difficult to buy into the separate *me* story.

As the myth of the personal self, with its history of pleasures and pains, starts to open, it will be revealed that the center of that which was taken to be substantial is in fact empty. It is at this time that the discriminative faculties of mind begin to sharpen. One can see that as mind arises, it is just a passing state and the potency once given to this bound energy field begins to lose its power.

Interdependence

Nature, with its mystery, wonder and deep, silent beauty is one of the greatest healers and teachers. Regular, mindful walks in nature can begin a deeper looking into ourselves, a deeper looking into the mysteries and interconnectedness of all of life. It cannot be stressed enough how a simple walk alone in a park, by the water or lake or just around the neighborhood, passing by the gardens and houses, passing by the parks with all its activity can be restorative to the soul. When walking, bring awareness to the feel of the feet on the pavement, the swing of the arms, the movement of breath — stay with the raw sensations. Once relaxed and merging with the flow of the walk, allow gratitude to well up from the heart, gratitude for all that is so freely given: the air, the warm sun or cool breeze, the laughter of children playing in the park, the smile of a passerby — all manifesting in the moment because life *is*. Breathe in gratitude on inspiration and on expiration, breathe out a prayer of "thank you" to God for the miracles that have brought about this moment and this opportunity to be mindful.

When walking, notice the feel of the environment. Is it early spring? Are the small buds beginning to manifest on the trees? Is it mid-winter after a rain? Are the raindrops hanging like diamond earrings from the bare branches? If one is drawn to a tree, the water or a garden, stop awhile and breathe it in. Stay awhile as if one has all the time in the world. If there is a bench or stairway near, sit down and relax, sit as one homeless, nameless, lacking possessions — like the heart of a renunciate. Sit as if uncertain about the next moment, yet unconcerned by it, as if there is nothing better to do... just this moment... this breath... this beautiful opportunity to see existence as it is.

When looking at a tree, a child or the water, observe it with innocence. Allow the veil of judgment and expectation to drop. See in the tree your own body. The roots firm in the soil where it gathers nutrients in an effortless manner, the trunk, the spreading branches reaching the heavens, soaking in the rain, the sun, the breeze, fully dependent, all interconnected. Sit with the tree in silence. Enjoy the majesty of the grace that is embodied in God's creations. Look deeply into the surroundings, the gardens, the humble grass, the bird perched on the branch... all moving in harmony, void of ego, opening up and blooming at just the right time, all beauty... all healing... all just right.

There is nothing better than the feel of being fully immersed in nature, fully taken in by its majesty and deep silence. And nature is so accessible, so open, so reliable — entirely void of judgment. Nature *is*. This practice of daily mindful walking has the potential to be deeply transforming. And nothing could be easier... just step out the door...

Make your life a living prayer

Treat every moment, every breath, every experience as sacred. Whether one is shopping, driving, walking, talking to a child or a loved one, cleaning the house, preparing dinner, sitting, whatever the activity, treat it with great care and respect. Breathe in the experience and allow it to become one with you.

Self-talk

Some positive self-talk is good and can bring one back to their senses for a brief period when the mind has wandered off onto a tangent, but this method is by means to be relied upon solely without spiritual guidance and practices in place.

Continual struggle with negative thoughts can often fuel them as well as decrease energy and increase isolation and depression. This is why one is encouraged to meditate, observe the breath and mental phenomena without getting caught up in it. This helps to bring one into the moment and conserve energy, rather than dissipate energy in struggle. "Equanimity" means to observe without judgment and so we observe what arises in meditation and in daily life (sensation, thought and emotion) without preferences or distaste/aversion — all passing phenomena appearing like clouds against a vast, spacious sky.

The Middle Way

Maintain a balanced lifestyle. Extremes deplete or deprive the soul in one way or another.

Embrace the mystery

The universal soul and the workings of unconditional love are a mystery. Once one gives up the struggle of attempting to understand something that is beyond comprehension, then life can be enjoyed for the mystery and adventure it is.

Mind your own business

What is important is to maintain independent awareness — not in a manner that is divisive, but to draw the mind within, all the while maintaining awareness of the surroundings in a detached manner. Come back to the center of being when mind draws out into the other — other people's problems, other people's conversations, other people's habits, other people's process. Forget about the who — who is doing, who is behaving, who is hurting and flow... witness... stay in awareness. Be watchful of getting caught up in other's issues. One can only know their own process. Even if one is thinking of another, what is thought of is filtered through the personal field, so one can never know the other until the mind falls silent. Then the other is seen as related to the self and when the troubles of another are expressed there is great compassion that sees through the external layers and takes the one hurting into the heart without being tainted in any way. To stay steady with one's own process takes a very strong mind that has grown soft through surrender. The mind that is weak grabs onto every little trouble and drowns in it. There is no ability to process, no open space to absorb. If one is serious, then continued attempts should be made to come back to the self. Over time this practice will steady the mind.

Stop

Take even a minute here and there each day and... *stop*. Stop right where you are and look around. Take even two or three conscious breaths. Breathe in the environment, the colors, the sounds, the sights, the movement, the grace, the flow. This activity is really nice when walking to one's car in the morning. Stop. Look at the clouds for a moment, breathe in the fresh air, absorb the scene. Enjoy it. Drink it in. As the rose gives of its sweet scent, the garden of life eternally gives of its fine fragrance, so take advantage of it. Breathe it in... Stop.

Reading

Reading about the lives of Saints, Gurus and spiritual masters is a very good way of going deeper into the self (as long as one does not get caught in the intellectual aspect of reading). Allow the feel of the writing to come through. What will be seen is that all awakened beings teach very differently, but speak the same truth. There are so many excellent books available now from teachers of the truth: Ramana Maharshi, Ramakrishna, Yogananda, The Upanishads, St John of the Cross, St Therese of Lisieux, Thich Nhat Hanh — so many. Then there is the beautiful poetry of Rumi, Khalil Gibran, Krishnamurti — all out there, all speaking the same truth, coming from the same heart. Voices of the past and present flowing from the one essence, the perfume of the truth rising from the same flower. These spiritual books carry a very strong transmission. If one reads with awareness, with a silent, attentive mind, so much can be absorbed.

Satsang

Satsang is association with truth or company of the wise — spending time with others that are living examples of truth in action is a great aid to one's spiritual progress. It also teaches one about community, devotion and being of service.

Seva

The translation of Seva in Sanskrit is *string*, which means that we are all connected and to serve one is to serve the whole. Like Karma yoga, Seva is giving without attachment to the fruits; it is a giving back to the universe for all the blessings that have been given to our lives. To give back from the heart helps maintain balance and harmony within. Also, selfless giving fuels devotion, which helps to make the path one walks far smoother and effortless. Seva can be given in the form of money, work or gifts, but whatever the external form, it is the heart of devotion that truly matters; and this internal flame as it grows bright, will draw others near that are in need of its warmth.

It is not solely for another's benefit that we give — selfless giving manifests due to the truth that we are not separate, but of one heart, and to serve one is to bring a greater sense of selflessness to the whole, including ourselves, our family, our own children and the children to come.

Seva is a tool of the heart offered by the universe to help maintain balance or a flow of equal exchange. Like all other universal tools, it is protective in that it seeks to ensure that one does not become drained or lazy and expecting — sitting back and expecting another to do the work. When a service is given freely from the heart, one should turn within and share of this treasure. In this manner we service the whole, which not only aids ourselves and our children, but all of humanity. It is true that many times we need a helping hand, but as we begin to see clearer and are strengthened by this clarity, it is our responsibility to give back so that others can become strengthened and sustained. The more we nurture a spirit of Seva, it is a joy to help, to give what we can give, to offer what we can offer. It feels good inside and brings the most lasting joy and this joy so easily refreshes others around us. To help others and to give back is to help oneself and to clear one's own path.

A heart that is on fire with love jumps at the opportunity to help, without question of what may be lost and without concern about personal gain… as the recipient of such kindness blooms in the warmth of this kind of summer love, this one then is slowly transformed as well and also becomes a great refreshment to others. It is in this way that the garden of the universal soul gets tended to. This garden is here for all of us to enjoy and therefore needs the work of many hands pitching in.

As the internal vision clears and selfless love is increasingly manifest, one becomes quite naturally an example for others.

Self-inquiry

Allow the question, *What is this I?* to come from the heart and return to the heart where it will be absorbed by the substance of the universe and do its own work. *Is*-ness cannot be known intellectually, it can only be entered when the questioner falls away. It is the mind that attempts to divide what cannot be divided. It is the mind that creates distance — I am here and you are there. Just sit with is-ness. Don't put a wash of mind over it.

Don't separate yourself from it. Life is and that is all. It just is, plain and simple, IS.

What arises next is left open and not for you to answer. Leave it to God. This is the problem — the mind wants to jump to a solution, an answer, something linear that it can make sense of, but if the question is left alone, then what? Find out. Sit with the question. Be quiet with it. Consciousness will take care of the rest of it. If you find yourself making complexities out of self-inquiry, stop it for a time and just stay with the mantra and breathing.

If the answer arises spontaneously in meditation this is fine — but this question, *Who am I?* gets a little tricky as the mind wants to immediately jump to a logical answer like, "Well, I am so and so with this and that qualities," which only further roots mental identifications. Self-questioning is meant to be dropped into the great pool of consciousness and allowed to sit and settle, and then just observe whatever bubbles arise — these bubbles give clues to mental holdings as well as bring up the mysteries of universal truths that are inherent in the being.

Self-inquiry, when given time to settle in stillness, will bring flashes of insight that will reflect back to the mind what is self (universal) and non-self (personal) and aid in pulling the non-self coverings away, if one can remain still — quiet, observing... allowing and offering the question for God to answer.

Self-inquiry is not used to further the thought process, but to help withdraw the mind and bring the scattered movement of mind into its center. A question such as *"What is this I?"* or *"Who am I?"* is posed to the self; this question should be then left alone to do its own work. Answers to the mysteries of life do not come through thought, but appear like a flash… an insight or revelation that is not of words.

Self-inquiry need only be used when the mind is active. When the mind quiets down, rest there and allow this stillness to darken, to deepen until the individual with his/her little troubles are unrecognizable in this depth. If you find that self-enquiry is stirring more thoughts, then stop and do the breathing. Always return to simplicity if one is confused or uncertain. Emotions are potentially cleansing in their pure state... no need to run them away. Relax into them, remaining fully present and awake. This energy used in running away from ourselves is very useful fuel that when concentrated into the moment can turn a small spark into a fire that will fully purify the internal view, then one can see mind, emotion, etc. for what it truly is — empty, vacant... something with no power in itself.

Surrender

Begin by not thinking about surrender and how it's done — let the whole thing go. Live by intuition like one who is blind, yet trusting of the one in charge of his care. Allow the heart to lead. Sit outside with the spacious sky all about, the wandering clouds, the wind, the birds. Enter into life with a heart of giving instead of wanting to take... to find something in it. Let the story of the seeker go. There is no one to surrender to — if anything, one surrenders to the self. Be still and allow the internal unfolding... as the flower yields to the warmth of the spring sun, its petals open in time with nature — in harmony with it. Such is the way of awareness — it is like the light of the sun and will in time unfold the mysteries of life, leaving the pure flow... empty, yet stunningly beautiful, dissolved of the sense of *me and mine*. Moving everywhere, yet going nowhere... this is-ness *is*.

To truly surrender one needs to first let down the guard...

Mantra

Mantra — to go beyond the suffering mind

Ommmmmmmmmmmmmmmmmm

When the mind is running in the day, going over the same ground, the mantra, *Om*, can be said internally or externally. Allow the vibration of the mantra to resonate in the heart center and move through the heart, dissolving into deep silence. Rest in the silence for as long as possible. Om can be said internally, in the midst of activity, or while sitting in meditation, especially at the beginning (to help draw one inward). The vibration of the mantra breaks up the energy patterns of mind. Follow the mantra through from beginning, middle to end.

A goal can only be fulfilled with continued perseverance —

so keep going...

So simple

The tools given by the master are very simple and the mind being so complex cannot trust that such naked simplicity has any potency, any power to aid in transformation. The teacher can only bring one as far as the being is willing to yield. If doubt, suspicion and stubbornness are perpetually entertained, the gate remains closed — not by the will of God, but by the seeker's determined, habitual reliance on the personal identity (ego) as guide and the lack of willingness to let go, if even for a moment. It is the ego that wants a *quick fix*, a *bigger and better*. It is the ego that wants eternal personal pleasure. When the simplicity of truth is offered, something so sweet, so selfless, so pure and innocent — as open as the green valley, as omnipresent as air — it is the determined egoic mentality that eventually declines this offering of the universe. *How will this serve me?* the ego asks, and it is this private hope of individual pleasure or power that so easily moves one off course and back into the material world with its personal pleasure and pain.

The head cannot understand the workings of the heart, the timing of the heart or the view of the heart. It is the universal life force embodied in the awakened being that manifests as a potential passage to the *one heart* - to help one through the maze and bramble of the egoic world. Pointings are given as signposts to tell the seeker, *not this way, not this way... yes, this is the way...*

It is through direct experience that there is a knowing, an understanding, a communion, a direct experience of the mysteries. The universal force moves through the channels, clearing the narrow mentality that has bound one to the world of the material and as the sludge is dissolved, spirit becomes increasingly manifest. This clearing process takes place in the embodied state as spirit is not this or that — it is not bound — it is here in the physical form and remains when the form falls away. It is eternal and not dependent on form, but form depends on it. Just as the aura of the small bud appears before the physical manifestation of the little bud, spirit is present before, during and after the physical. The physical is not the end all, the be all, the wisdom.

The spiritual path need not be approached in complexity. Come into yourself. Come into the being and walk it in a simple manner, like a child who does not know anything and is totally dependent on what is around. A young child does not care how the food arrived in front of him; he just eats it. He does not care if the home is big, small or cluttered — he just feels good being warm and loved. He has no caring and makes no distinction about the personal appearance of the caregiver, but simply responds to the guidance, to the love given, and basks in it, plays in it, rejoices in it. To throw the burden of personal responsibility down does not mean one becomes irresponsible, but to mentally give God the burden to take care of and trust a little. Allow the next moment to unfold. Observe it with wonder. As most have seen, what needs to get done, does, whether we grind away internally at it or just allow the next moment to unfold — all the same (*the hard way or the harder way*, as my Guru puts it). Surrender spares one the course of the harder way.

Meditation

Take some time each day to sit (even for five minutes). If there is a refreshing, quiet place in the home, this is great, if not, one might consider creating one. It takes very little time or effort. A vase of flowers and a picture of a respected teacher, some incense and a few pieces from nature that one connects with. Sit in a comfortable manner, keeping the spine straight. Slowly bring awareness to the breath. Come back to the breath when mind wanders. This is all that needs to be done. Relax fully into the experience.

What does it feel like to just be?

Some that live alone may complain they are so lonely, they cannot meditate for the mind is taken over with being alone and restless with the search to gain love somewhere outside of the self. Then there are those that complain that it is difficult to meditate because of relationship and there are yet others that complain about children being a distraction. If one can look at the picture in a general way, then what is seen is that it is mind that is the barrier, not the situation.

The circumstances that come to us are due to karma, which is grace — it is God's mercy offered, a chance to relive a lesson as a means to deepen understanding and compassion. The experiences that come do not have some deep, personal meaning to them, but are more like an offering — a chance to look into and see ourselves clearer... what comes is never because of someone else, but an unfolding of the journey within. Our partner, child or friend is looking for the exact same things we are — to be safe, to be loved, to be happy and to be held by mother — the universal giver, the one who loves unconditionally. Of course, the loved one may not completely understand this universal desire due to the longing being buried for a time, so temporarily it may seem as if the paths are out of sync.

If one looks deeper at those with whom we are most intimate, in a quiet way, without judgment, without hoping the loved one might change or imposing mind on them, there is a change that takes place immediately — a softening. One can say to themselves about another, I was like that once, so I understand

— I have walked that way before at some point, but we are of the same light (something I have said internally more than once about my sixteen-year-old).

We have been offered so many chances, again and again forgiveness has come which is grace... this moment is grace. It is a miracle to enjoy even one moment without the shadow of judgment (which are simply shields to the heart). The more we relax and let go, we will find that we are no different than our brother, friend, partner or child. This heart of union can only be known when one risks being vulnerable... then we can see what we have termed the "other" is our own being, expressing, changing, growing, learning, loving, hoping, dreaming... the flow of life expressing itself.

Meditation has its roots in life, not away from it. It is simple to begin. I started as a single mom with a baby, there was nothing fancy about it — nothing was needed but myself. So to begin, just breathe into the heart and relax, begin to become aware, and soon, the world will take on a very different appearance.

Chapter 6

Meditation Exercises from Swami-G

Starting Practices

Balanced Breath Meditation/Shanti Mind Pranayam

This practice is quite safe and one you can put into place wherever you are at during the day. The advantage of this practice is that it allows the mind to begin to still, it brings one to center and allows one to relax with whatever stressors are coming up in the midst of life. This is a wonderful practice for those in the midst of a Kundalini awakening. It keeps bringing you to center, and whatever phenomena comes along the way (the Kundalini energy), it allows you to have some stability as a practice to come back to so that one can allow them to release.

Begin to relax the body…
Become aware of your breath…

Close your eyes…

Notice your breath may be coming from the upper chest…

As you begin to relax into this practice, you will notice that the breath begins to relax, the body begins to relax and the stomach begins to move like a bellows. When the stomach begins to move like a bellows and the rest of the body begins to relax then you will know you are making progress within this practice.

Allow the breath to become very natural…

Let the tension fall away…

When you start to become relaxed, put the focus on the air as it comes out of the nostrils. Notice as your attention begins to focus in that one side will have less airflow and the other side will have more airflow. When you can determine which side has less airflow put your attention on that side and consciously allow it to relax. When one is able to do this, the air should be coming evenly out of the nostrils. Once you get that even balanced breath, keep your awareness within that balance.

Dissolving Divisions

Here are two practices that are quick to learn. One raises the vibration and the other helps to break down the barrier between you and what you are viewing. Both of these practices are incorporated to bring you into that sense of Oneness.

I Am That I Am

When your eyes are closed and you are going into meditation, intone the mantra of "I AM That I AM." Do this out loud and this will help to send these vibrations throughout your body system and into your cellular body and the energy body as well.

Close the eyes and say:

"I AM That I AM, I AM That I AM, I AM That I AM, I AM That I AM, I AM That I AM, I AM That I AM, I AM That I AMMMMMMMMM... I AM That I AM, I AM That I AM, I AM That I AM, I AM That I AM, I AM That I AM, I AM That I AM, I AM That I AM, I AM That I AM, I AM That I AMMMMMMMM."

As you are doing this, say it from the heart. Keep your attention within the heart center.

Om That I Am

This practice is quite effective to begin to break down the barriers between you and other, to where you come into more alignment of the feeling of being as One.

Open your eyes and say:

"OM That I AM, OM That I AM, OM That I AM, OM That I AM, OM That I AM, OM That I AM, OM That I AM, OM That I AM, OM That I AM, OM That I AM, OM That I AMMMMMMMM."

Repeat this mantra while looking at whatever you see in front of you. If you have a partner, you can look into your partner's eyes and intone this "Om That I Am."

For videos and audio on these starting practices, visit www.GuruSwamiG.com.

The Path Beyond "I Am"

Do the following exercise to balance the emotions. Take as much time as needed on each part until you feel the desired results. If rushed, you will not achieve the results you wish to attain... Practice each day and then use as needed to maintain a healthy balance.

Find a comfortable place, whether in a chair in the house, or you may even feel the need to sit outside. ANY place where you feel comfortable and safe will do.

Breathe gently in and out until you start to feel a calming come over you. If music helps you to attain this state then feel free to use it. Once calmed and relaxed enough to focus proceed to the following exercise. Visualize and feel as much as possible for best results.

"I release into the ground despair, anger, hurt, depression, feeling of being worthless and unworthy, feelings of being unloved and unlovable, that they may be transformed. They are released with love and compassion."

"I draw in with each breath from the top of my head to the tips of my feet PEACE, JOY LOVE, EQUANIMITY, CREATIVE ENERGY, and LIFE MORE ABUNDANT. I allow these feelings to enter in and fill my being until I can hold no more..."

"I consciously hold PEACE, LOVE, JOY, ENERGY and COMPASSION, so that I may walk in balance this day."

Note: As needed stand and walk, feeling with each step the release of negative emotions. With each breath feel the influx of positive emotions. This will keep you conscious of keeping in balance throughout the day.

Open Eye Meditation

Begin with the balanced breath

Bring awareness to the feel of the breath

Moving in and out of the nostrils

Allow it to totally relax

Stay with this until the breath feels balanced

Allow the abdomen to soften

Allow the muscles to relax

When ready, bring the attention to the right side of the chest

This is the home of the spiritual heart

Which is not a physical location, but a cognition of Being

It is a place that develops awareness purely

Relax into the spiritual heart...

Allowing the breath to breathe itself...

Soften into this presence for a time

If the mind wants to focus on a particular object

Soften the gaze around the object

Allow awareness to expand from within the Heart outward

Not focusing on anything in particular

Not concerned about anything particular

Now, relax in the Spiritual Heart Center

Float in the fullness of awareness

Allow all barriers to fall

So that it is open to the totality of the

Universe as ONE

Sounds come

Sounds go

The body relaxed

The gaze softened

No concerns

No clinging

No aversion

Just warmth radiating from

The Center of Being

This is seeing through the Heart

This is the open eye meditation

It can be done throughout the day

An unfolding meditation

Pick a place where you will not be disturbed and where you feel totally safe and secure. Pick a meditation type of music such as flute, rhythmic drums, electronic, or perhaps a CD or tape of nature sounds. You may even do this exercise outdoors at the beach or at any other place where you feel safe and undisturbed. (If music or nature sounds are distracting you may just sit quietly and concentrate on focused breathing.) You may sit in a chair, on the floor or on the ground in a comfortable position. Relax by breathing gently in and out, while coming into sync with the music or nature sounds.

When you have reached a slowing of outside stimuli, begin to allow all stress, worries and negativity to start moving down through the body and out into the ground. Breathing gently and calmly, start to allow and feel your senses becoming ever more open. See yourself as a flower, which starts as a bud and slowly opens with the warmth of the sun to become a radiant, colorful and fragrant flower... Now start to explore the color the brilliance of how it looks. Explore how the color feels. Is it warm or cool? How does it make you feel? What does it project to yourself and to others? Now start to explore the fragrance. Is it sharp or sweet? How does it affect you and others by its fragrance? Allow yourself to merge with the flower and to sense its life and its purpose. Does it have emotions and feelings? What wisdom does it convey to you and teach you? Give thanks to the flower for sharing with you its knowledge and kindness...

Now it is time to move onto other experiences. The universe is yours to explore and to gain wisdom from and to merge with... Learn to feel the connection to all plants, animals, peoples and earth. Once connected, move out into the universe and to God the Great Spirit, which gives all Life, Light and Love... Be always grateful, loving and kind and know that we are always connected to the universe and that we never stand alone in a vacuum.

Chapter 7

Spiritual Teachers and Masters

Through example, word and deed — God-realized saints manifest to deliver this message to a suffering humanity: fear not, for death cannot touch you — it is an illusion — you are eternal — you are already whole — the core of humanity is good — all is well — be happy and rejoice.

We are not separate individuals; we are one with the heart of being. We are conscious beings totally dependent on the life-giving forces of the universe, totally dependent on the supreme, intelligent force that works through the form... that works through the mind. We are all guided by the light of intuition (some are just more in tune with this intuitive force than others), all needing the nourishment that the universe offers in the form of food, air, water and beyond this, the nourishment offered to the spirit that holds and feeds one — the inherent wealth of pure nutrition that is eternal, the pure waters of the universal soul that sustains all of life. On this we are sustained, whether we are aware of it or not.

We are not independent; we are one in spirit and to experience this transforming aspect of our being, the divine inner beauty that shines on through all experience — to directly enter union with the source of all of life, one needs guidance. All supreme beings — all saints, all spiritual masters — received help at one point or another along the way from a Sat Guru... a Master... an Awakened Priest... a Bodhisattva... a Mahatma... a Holy One... a Saint. A true spiritual master holds one steady internally while aiding in pulling away the coverings that hide the light of God... that cover the true being, that keep one feeling separate from the eternal. A true spiritual master helps one stand on their own two feet until the soul eventually does not need assistance — having become the beloved, having entered union with the source, all then takes place on its own — there is no other, just God. This one will then be a light to the world, in whatever capacity that manifests. It can be no other way for all moves with pure intelligence when the ego is dissolved. This is the movement of the supreme self. This is the true nature that resides in all hearts, flowing unobstructed, void of self-consciousness, embodying the divine mother — nature, silent and perfect. This presence that is all healing brings nourishment to the soul that opens itself to it. Like the empty cup that receives the cooling rains from the heavens or the open arms that welcome the innocent love of a child, the one that is welcoming, that is receptive, that is open, will receive this blessing. This eternal offering of the *one heart* that is here to warm the being to its inherent light.

"Guru is the knowledge that acts like a ladder to the upper realms, is a raft to carry you across safely the torrid eddies of mental states." — Swami-G

The only true way of recognizing a spiritual master is through the heart. It is a connection of love that is mutually nourishing. When the internal vision is cleared enough through surrender to the continual ache that burns in the throat and heart with a longing to return to source... to return home, this one knows the great soul immediately and is drawn towards this light like one who has lost their way and has been wandering for a very long time through a wilderness without substantial sustenance. Wandering, wandering, seeking shelter and finally, after such a long time, there is a light — a fire burning in the distance that one draws near without hesitation. This is the light of the universal soul. The one who has been made soft by suffering, by laying down the petty ways of the world, by prayer, by laying bare the narrow, personal self, by allowing the elements to work on one. The soul that has exhausted the paths leading to personal fulfillment, that is ripe with love — ripe with the ache to know, turns immediately towards this warmth. It is in this relationship that begins as dual in nature (within the seeker), that the master, through transmission and pointings, pushes one toward the internal Guru. The true seeker offers little resistance to this force, just remains open, observant, calm and steady through the shifting states. The internal Guru pulls one from the inside and there is this play, this working that is one in spirit, one with the aim of the universe: to unite with the true Self (non-dual consciousness or Christ consciousness).

> *"It is all within, the Guru without only connect one to the ever-present Guru." — Swami-G*

Don't expect the master to conform to personal expectations. The beauty of spirit is that it does not conform; it is much freer than that. It moves in relationship to what is needed and when one is caught in the fetters of mind, *one does not know what is needed, having never traversed any other ground...* so the master will blow out the narrow outlook born of ego, the individual desires of wanting something to be a certain way, of expecting something to behave according to the personal desire — all of which hold one to a certain stance, a certain view that creates stagnation. A true master does not place intentional boundaries between themselves and the student. A true master does not distance themselves from the ones that are hungering for the truth. The *one heart* is accessible, open, welcoming yet doing whatever it takes to bring one to the highest awareness — even if it means tough love — whatever it takes. This is the movement of pure consciousness. The true master will say, "I am what you are" and directly embody this experience by the intimacy of expression. There will be a human quality, yet a transcendence, an openness to life, yet an authority. Certainly, being in the presence of the Guru should bring a rest, a peace, a feeling of progress and expanded feeling that may or may not occur immediately. Trust the pull of the heart and not the head. Though there are many teachers in life, it is best to remain with one master. Truth is one. Guru is one. Love is one... this is the flow of the universe. Remaining true to one sincere master will prevent imbalance, speed progress, aid surrender, help deepen commitment and fortitude, help bring about humility — all very important, if one is truly interested in transcendence.

> *"The Guru is not a person. Guru is a reality that penetrates all of existence." —Swami-G*

The master will appear when the student has prepared for this grace. In the meantime, it is wise to begin to prepare and to make a start — to very slowly take some steps. Start right where you are; there is nothing else needed — all will fall into place in time.

Guru/Chela relationship

It is only the divine eye that rests like a jewel in the center of the flower of being surrounded and nourished on the roots of faith that can see through the difficulties the Guru/Chela relationship might bring — drawing on that internal knowing that what has come is a cleansing that can never be anything but grace.

The Guru/Chela relationship is a love story of the purest sort. It is not uncommon for the Guru to know the true chela immediately as if this great one has been waiting for the student to come and knows him, like a mother would know her own child that has returned after a long absence. It is a joyful reunion and there is an immediate divine eternal bond that takes place. The chela that is ripe puts up little, if any, resistance to the purification process offered by the Guru and is eventually washed clean of all personal motive or mistaken sense of a false, separate self. The feeling, as the relationship blossoms, is as if both teacher and student are like one person, revealing over time within the student, the same selfless aim — to bring those who are willing into the singular universal light that is of one heart.

This relationship is grace blossoming under just the right conditions and maturation, like a rare flower that over lifetimes of nourishment through suffering and pure desire finally breaks through, drawing the loved object towards its center, dissolving the feel of two into its sweet essence. There are many accounts written of the Guru/Chela bond. A very well written account is a book by Swami Yogananda in *Autobiography of a Yogi*. Yogananda expresses so beautifully the love relationship of this bond and also speaks so well to the dedication, commitment, devotion and surrender that are needed to stay steady within it.

The heart that is pure holds this blessed, rare relationship very dear and is not inclined in the least to stray.

When one expects the master to arise like a vision of perfection that will instantly wash clean all accumulated suffering and karma and bow to the disciple pleasing him in every way, then there is great disappointment when internal challenge arises and the student is pulled into looking at themselves and told to make consistent efforts towards their own progress.

A true Guru takes responsibility for the disciple's life, is an advisor, a protector — like a very strict, yet loving parent that is eternally helping the seeker to stand on his/her own — to be a light unto themselves. Oftentimes the more ethical the master, the fewer the disciples they have as these great ones do not cater to ego, but exist and express themselves in a manner of which the primary aim is to cut away at the illusive coverings of mental conditionings that keep one bound to the physical reality — only the very dedicated seeker that has prepared for this grace has the endurance to remain in a relationship such as this. My Guru, Swami-G, is such a teacher and the ones that have made quick judgments about her see only the outer coverings and fall away quickly after receiving her straightforward counsel.

The master will without fail quicken the spiritual progression of the student who has prepared the way to receive or at least is willing to listen and surrender, but if the heart and mind are closed, willful, demanding, suspicious and expectant or the mind is very weak, lacking endurance, then even the master cannot help a one that is not willing or has not prepared.

To receive the truth, one needs to take time to become intimate with its light, which may be strong at first, but the sincere chela stays steady until the internal eyes and heart slowly grow accustom to this new climate and then the terrain begins to feel natural — native — like one was meant to be surrounded by this universal guide that once intimately known is revealed as nothing but the truest, highest form love and affection.

When one dismisses the ordinary existence looking for bigger and better experiences then the Buddha, or awakened one, is missed, but when one comes fully into the everyday life, looking deeply with a sincere desire to know, it is then that the master appears and very soon all of life appears as the Buddha.

When a teacher manifests that is dedicated to bringing humanity to the truth, it is in the seekers' best interest to not dismiss it readily or take it casually, but to spend time fueling the fire of devotion (bhakti), love, surrender and gratitude — to attune themselves to this divine force that will offer the highest protection and counsel. This takes dedicated work and effort on the student's part. The true student that puts in time towards this divine relationship should feel challenged because without this intense energy, there is no growth — one should feel like they are working at coming outside of their habits and ways — that they are putting forth energy towards the heart and fueling the spirit of satsang (the association with truth — the group and community of truth). If one feels challenged and is having a hard time with this, then it can be looked at as tapas, like an austerity as a way to move beyond mental and physical attachments. Faith, trust and love are the ingredients that help one to see that whatever the situation or challenge — when there is this gift of divine protection, then one can rise to the challenge and know that what is offered is for one's growth — to fuel the heart of humility and surrender.

The master comes in all shapes, forms and temperaments to suit the needs of the time and can appear very ordinary on the outside. It is only those that have a strong desire to see beyond the externals that will notice the internal invisible treasure when it appears and can partake of its riches.

The Guru's ways can be harsh as well as very tender and filled with joy, love and playfulness — all of which I have witnessed in being near my Guru as well as being in the presence of other divine beings. I have also read and heard about many saints and sat in the presence of some that make Swami-G look tame as she is extremely understanding and lenient of Western ways and traditions. She can move within tradition and non-tradition. She is well-versed in the Hindu scriptures as well as the teachings of Christ and the power of truth shines equally in each when she is discussing them. It is best then to not have a pre-conceived idea about the master for this relationship is a wondrous mystery. The blessing received by coming to know a spiritual master is transmitted for the most part in a non-verbal manner through the initiation of silence (mounadiksha). There have been many incidents where just sitting near Swami-G while she was typing the mails, having lunch or shopping with her, the mind would still and there would be waves of blissful energy that infused the being — this is the beauty and light that is given to the one that stays steady and becomes intimate with this selfless offering given by the universe.

The master may have sat by you today, walked by you or talked to you today, but you did not know it because your cup was so full, his majesty could not share of his drink — the sweet nectar of truth.

Always be prepared for the unexpected...

Renunciation

To nurture the heart of a renunciate is what truly matters, the outerwear, the ceremonies are meant for some, but to give up internal contradiction and grasping and live within that inner peace of aloneness — an aloneness that is full and welcomes life — this is what matters.

Spiritual initiation solidifies a deep commitment to know God. It bonds one to a lineage of completed masters which carries a very strong transmission and aids in pulling one beyond mind into a consciousness that is universal.

A Hindu renunciate is called a Sannyasi or sadhu (sadhvi is female) which literally means, "abandoning," "throwing down" or "to lay down." A Hindu monk is an ascetic or practitioner of yoga. Traditionally the sannyasi, after being initiated, will take his begging bowl and live the life of a hermit, wandering and begging for food at dusk. The sadhu renounces all worldly thoughts and desires and fully immerses the self in meditation and contemplation of God. The religious practices of a sadhu are varied and can be quite austere for some, but if done with sincerity, these practices help to burn off individual karma as well as the karma of the community at large. The renunciate is solely dedicated to moksha (liberation).

Sannyasa has an external meaning that is rich with symbology. The head is shaved as a symbol of giving up worldly attachments. There is the wearing of white robes initially, meaning one is dead to the world, then one changes into orange robes which symbolizes the burning away of samskaras or past conditionings. Rudraksha mala beads are worn which are symbolic of the tears of the Hindu deity, Shiva's compassion. A pandit or Hindu scholar leads the ceremony with chanting, which is repeated by all the initiates. After each chant, a rose petal is thrown into the dhuni (holy fire pit). There are various sitting postures, including full prostrations and then the spiritual names are given, which carry a very high charge, each one symbolizing union in one way or another, but each is individual and meant as a quality to deepen or move towards. These names are given out to the sannyasi by the Guru and with the Guru's blessing. The name of a Swami always ends in "ananda" which means "bliss" — so the full meaning is "the bliss of —" be it "the bliss of mental discrimination" (viveka), "the bliss of union" (yoga), "the bliss of pure love" (Prema), "the bliss of union with Brahman or pure consciousness" (Swarupa), "the bliss of fulfillment" (Siddha). The energy present in the symbolic expression represented in the ceremony is very strong, as the material has absorbed the high vibration of the ritual of meditation and Shakti. This is why the effort put towards sadhana benefits the entire community and moves out into the world. This energy of pure consciousness, as well as loving intent, is soaked up by matter and literally changes the energy field of the environment — all a very good thing.

Religious garments and symbols are meant as outer expressions of the internal journey. If the heart is not sincere in truly desiring to know God, religious attire loses its meaning. It is much better to seek God inwardly with pure intention and to wear ordinary clothes — to be anonymous, to be nameless — than to don religious robes and a spiritual name without sincerity. A Swami, as my dear Guru puts it, is a "function" — it is not about a personality; it is not to be used to prop up the ego, as a way to secure power or material gain: the ceremony, the name, the robes are to be seen as expressions of the wondrous internal journey — a journey that is universal and open to all.

In the Western world, the atmosphere is not suitable to wander as a monk — this is true for males, but is especially true for females. It is not safe to build a fire, to sit outside and go up to homes begging for meals in the evening. In India, the wandering sannyasis are primarily male — for it is also dangerous there to roam at night alone as a female. Swami-G offered the ceremony here in the West for dedicated students who were drawn towards the life of a renunciate as a way to deepen practice and eventually achieve moksha. A sannyasa, in this case, is a householder — still very much involved in the work world — the world of family and regular routine, but continues these ordinary activities absorbed in sadhana.

Spirituality is not separate from life. This is the main piece of wisdom that should be understood. It is not something that only takes place in a far off land, nor does it need a special environment, special clothing, a special form or background — it is now, it is in the moment. It is cooking dinner, washing clothes, making beds, raising children — the routine of work with phones, meetings and continual interruptions... it is the breath, the heartbeat — it is. This is the beauty of spirit: that it is not here or there, but ever present, without conditions and without constraints. To realize the simplicity of this *beingness* one needs to just begin to be fully present — which can be done anytime, anywhere.

Endnote

"I'm so stupid, I don't know I'm stupid.

That is how stupid I am."

$E=MC^2$ — *"What in the world does that mean?"*

The quotes above came from me spontaneously years ago, prior to meeting my Guru. I did not understand what I was saying at the time, but could see easily after meeting her that together these statements speak to the path of awakening: from ignorance to bliss — from hell to heaven — from darkness to light. From a state where one does not realize the confinements they are caught in due to the chronicity of the predicament and lack of clear light to a state where all is light, boundless, free and full of possibility.

Kundalini

When kundalini bloomed in full in my late thirties, I prayed and prayed to be returned back to my normal way of being, which was at least known to me. Where was this unfamiliar reality leading me anyway? I will tell you this — that the first time the mind stills every burning question such as this is answered and the first time samadhi is entered, one is in love forever with the divine. This is where the path of the mystic leads — towards direct experience where all roads of the seekers meet — in union and full rejoicing.

Swami-G is probably the most outspoken regarding the kundalini process that I have read or heard about. This process is one that requires clear direction and very intimate connection with the seeker, as one can get lost so readily in the psychic phenomena and shifting states of consciousness that manifest. This clarity and direct, personal guidance is what Swami-G has brought to humanity, which does not mean that all are ready for her service, but for those that are, it is a great boon. The purpose of this book is not to detail kundalini, but to help the seeker to begin on the path and to share with the world that the Guru will come when one is ready — to not worry. To believe and trust that the right guidance will come at the right time and that it is better to begin than to settle for mundane consciousness — there is so much more.

I would also like to urge seekers not to chase after kundalini or attempt to open it, as this can be a very unsettling experience without proper guidance. When one has a competent guide and the proper spiritual foundation is laid, kundalini opens gently as one roots themselves to the eternal; the shifts that come up cannot toss one around so easily. This is the blessing of coming under proper guidance. Kundalini is a great boon — a cleansing — a very legitimate form of yoga that can, if navigated properly, speed up spiritual progression and bring one to union in just one lifetime.

If the reader is interested in exploring kundalini further, it is advised to not delve deeply into the biology of kundalini — to not focus on chakras and powers, but to understand that it is a journey through consciousness, that it is intended to clear debris on all levels and bring one to a higher state of consciousness and eventually the bliss of God union.

"Kundalini from Hell to Heaven" written by Ganga Karmokar (Swami-G) is available for those who want to know the true facts about this process. Swami-G explains kundalini in detail and also offers tools to navigate safely through this journey, but again it cannot be said enough that one needs a competent guide to come to completion.

Realization

Sage Swami Siddhananda-Puri entered full realization July 20, 2007 in the presence of her Beloved Guru Swami-G. Below is an e-mail correspondence between Guru and Chela during the final days of this transformation.

Siddhananda: *Last night beheld more of the universe than ever before ... a total black engulfing the body, could not see or hear it felt — the body would react in fear sometimes — a shuddering of the limbs or drawing away, but not the mind. Then blips of a simplicity beyond what was felt before — I don't know why anyone would be called a sage — it is so utterly simple, so just being self — a few times had to laugh.*

Guru: *Hahahaha, closer and closer — the final edge is near. And YES it is complete and Utter Simplicity. Complexity hides its Pure Beauty.*

Siddhananda: *Well, off to work ... the river of life carrying the body along, but am not going anywhere ... aaahh life is beautiful in its is-ness. To live the poem is very different.*

Guru: *Yes — the living breathing poetry in motion — Life.*

The self alone is.

Om,

Siddhananda

One in the garden of Lila.

Endnote

God Consciousness

Within that which is whole
there are no shadows
the play of now has come into being
and life is full in glory

behold the light that seeks no other
what you are
you have always been
within the heart of the truth
that is the flower of this moment

Seek me here
find that which does not cover
in the seed
of perfection
arising
arising
singing
joy

Home is the within
that has no belongings
he who carries the burden long
and laboring
will not find it

come linger here
in the garden of beauty

that seeks no other
thou wanders out of the holy palace
into the streets of knowing
but hurry not out
this time

come
live within the freedom of now
you are this
and can be no other

love is the seed
that does not look outside
it rests secure in the heart
containing the mysteries of all creation
when blooming
unlocks knowledge
as it knows nothing but truth

Breathe in the moment
sing of no other
as you are this single beating heart
where did you get a different knowing?

The garden of truth grows one flower
that dances eternally alone
in glory and in song

Can I show you?

Can I show you the deepest blue ocean
where waves do not reach
only the quiet depths of the soul sit
reflecting each small bit of life
even one grain of sand

Will you fly with me through heaven
on a clear night
with the lone bird that circles
swoops and dives with nothing
to hem it in
a still motion dance

Will you journey with me down the path
that opens up a visual wonder
the trees, blue sky and clouds
the child on the street corner
the woman in the pink dress
picking flowers
the empty beauty that runs
through each piece of it
unfolding joy

Will you warm yourself with this light
that is offered
and bask within it
forgetting all cares
Softening those crinkles on the brow

that have come
from attempting to understand

Will you forget with me awhile
what the whole game is about
and sit with your knees drawn up
like child
drinking in the moment
knowing your are loved
for just being

Beauty Only

Oh love
the cloud that hides
the glorious mountain top
has now vanished
and in the heart
beauty shines

In the thick of the forest
in the open valley
at the foot of the mountain
and rushing crowd of the city
in the heart
beauty shines

In thought
in the dance of nothingness
in the smile and tear
in the mother
the father
the friend
the stranger
and the beggar by the roadside
in the heart
beauty shines

the cloudy day
the sun breaking through
the tender leaf

the drop of dew trembling
the simple blade of grass
so simple is the holy consciousness
shining on all
revealing beauty only

The seasons come and go
the child grows quickly
and the body gathers aches
yet within the holy consciousness
nothing changes
nothing moving
coming or going
only the beauty of truth
revealed in all that passes
transcending all
living in all
beauty shining

Drop the silk veil

see through my eyes

live like no other

breathe the first breath

breathe the warm sun

feel the hard earth

burn in the fire

get lost in the clouds

just breathe...

lose yourself

breathe

lose yourself

fly like a bird

free up the soul

soar without wings

cover your eyes

live in the heart

live in the heart

just breathe

lose yourself

breathe

lose yourself

Life is Water

I don't know if I exist

and all is well

Sweet love has cast its spell

and there is nothing that I miss

drinking in the wine of eternity

this soul is no more

and all is well

there is nothing that I miss

swimming in the ocean of bliss

swimming in the ocean of bliss

You told me all was sweet

when the heart is open

now my beloved

you and I meet

I am gone but you

live on

This is heaven's kiss

heaven's kiss

I am this ocean

though it meets the shore

Life is water

always the open door

The tongue forever singing God's song

Om, Om, Om

this journey so long

and there is nothing I miss

Swimming in the ocean of bliss

Swimming in the ocean of bliss

Life is water

Life is water

drink it in

drink it in

Swimming in the ocean of bliss

Swimming in the ocean of bliss

Bliss

Joy

Love

I am

Ommmmmmmm

Blessed is the Womb

blessed is the womb
that gives rise to the babe of freedom
on wings of song
in the open where nothing is hidden
bright moment in time
the darkness dissipates in the substance that always is
sweet nectar
pouring forth like a river
from the heart

the truth carries a fragrance
that is the blooming of NOW
fresh with innocence as if seeing for the first time
divine light that sheds itself without distinction

the flower is my soul that lights itself in glory
the open space this heart that shuts nothing out
the rolling hills the waves of bliss that rise and fall gently
the sky this pristine consciousness sparkling
the bird's call the joy that rises spontaneously
the darkness the void filled with flowing life
the earth the ground of being steady and unwavering

myself to sing of thee is to find sweet stillness
to know thee is to be empty

to love is to release that which is not pure

holy is this ONE

where there is no meeting

only the dance of 0

the eternal song of IS

Nameless and formless am I
fresh as the spring breeze
joyful as the bubbling brook
as open as the deep valley
as stable as the mountain
changeless and timeless am I

no arms can hold me
no doors can shut me out
no walls can contain me

I seek no home
for there is none
bare and open
vulnerable in fullness I am

The long storm has ground me
to nothing
and the dust has blown away
across the sea
across the land of coming and going
now life can play
in its fullness

Come
be that which you have always been
thou will be as welcome

as the new dawn and

the fresh spring breeze

thou will find the open beauty

that the sages sing of

timeless and unchangeable

the jewel in the heart

This is the song of the love

that seeks no other

Om

Love the dance that is yourself
never departing, but always finding itself HERE
breathe in the fragrance that is yourself
as the music has never stopped
it is endless like the ocean that is
forever singing of life

there is nowhere that love will not be
when the love is true
not colored by something other
or caught in a net of fantasy
love will be the essence that is uncovered
that has spoke of itself to you for so long
like the wind is felt on the face
and the feet feel the sweet earth
this call has always been

turn towards the sound that sings of no other
truth will be found there
like a jewel that has never been tucked away
but always out there in openness and joy
singing of itself in glory
as the trees spread its branches far and wide
and the moon reflects its light on the still lake
as the mountain sits strong and steady
and the bird sings without restraint to the morning light

truth is HERE

and is forever singing its song

in silence

May all beings be happy

there is a knowing within

that will return one home

as easily as the river finds the sea

as easily as the bud gives rise to the flower

as easily as the leaf falls with wind

and spirals to the soft earth

as easily as the child finds the mother in the crowd

as easily as the water flows down the mountain

and the rains plop on the green leaves

as easily as the sun reflects on the still lake

there is a knowing within

that will return one home

Glossary

Ananda: Bliss. The pure joy, ecstasy or entasy or God-consciousness or spiritual experience. In its highest sense, ananda is expressed in the famous Vedic description of God: Sat Chit Ananda — existence, consciousness, bliss. The divine or superconsciousness mind of all souls.

Anava: The veil of duality: a state of consciousness wherein there is a sense of *I* and *mine* — separation from the Divine. One of the three Buddhist malas or bondages: anava, karma and maya.

Bhakti Yoga: The path of devotion and surrendering until the ego is totally effaced. Union with love.

Bodhi-mind: Awakened mind. Bodhi is a Sanskrit word for awakening or enlightenment. Buddha found enlightenment while meditating under a Bodhi tree.

Brahman: Absolute. The root source and divine ground of everything that exists: the unchanging, infinite, immanent and transcendent reality, which is the Divine ground of all things in the universe.

Chi: The vital force believed in Taoism and other Chinese thought to be inherent in all things. The unimpeded circulation of chi and a balance of its negative and positive forms in the body are held to be essential to good health in traditional Chinese medicine.

Chela: The spiritual disciple of a Guru.

Conditionings: The habitual reactive response to stimuli based on the identification and attachment with the body and the sense of an inward entity programmed into our consciousness during and continuing into adulthood and covering over our true identity as the self.

Doership: The illusion of a separate sense of self as the doer, through effort, creating karma, and demonstrating an ignorance of the Divine Doer, and a lack of surrender.

Dhuni: A sacred fire pit. It is tended to by sadhus at their homes.

Ego: The external personality, the sense of *I* and *mine*; a separate sense of self, apart from God.

Energy Work: An ancient and sacred healing art that can create a deeply meditative and healing experience for body, mind and soul through a series of gentle but powerful infusions of concentrated life force energy, enhancing the body's inherent power to heal itself.

Equanimity: The state of being calm, stable, composed, especially under stress.

Global Karma: Collective karma of humanity.

Grace: God working through man and not done by individual effort or with any sense of personal "doership."

Guru: Weighty one. A term that can be used to denote an authority on any given subject. Most commonly refers to one of spiritual knowledge. Refers to both the outer form of the Guru and the inner and ultimately supreme Guru. A Sat Guru is a spiritual preceptor.

Hinduism: Also known as "Sanatana Dharma" or the everlasting religion. Hinduism is not so much a religion as a way of life with the Universe as the center. Hinduism has a profusion of Gods and

Goddesses that are worshipped as manifestations of the supreme God, Brahman (the unchanging, infinite, transcendent reality).

Jiva: The individual soul, during its embodied state, bound by the three malas (or roots): karma, anava, maya.

Karma: Action or Act. The Universal law of action and reaction or cause and effect, and the fruits of those actions or subsequent effect returning to the one carrying out the deed. As you so sow so shall you reap.

Kundalini: The primordial cosmic energy lying dormant within every individual at the base of the spine, analogous to a coiled serpent. When aroused she enters the sushumna in the center of the spine, ascending to pierce each chakra or level of consciousness as she climbs to the crown chakra where Shakti unites with Shiva. To be completed Kundalini needs to come to rest within the Heart Center.

Lila: The play of God.

Lingam: The unmanifest — is used as a symbol for the worship of the Hindu God Shiva. It is the soul seed or pure consciousness containing within it the entire essence of the cosmos.

Mahatma: An honorific title meaning great soul, bestowed on particularly meritorious individuals.

Mantra: A religious or mystical syllable or poem, typically from the Sanskrit. They are intended to deliver the mind from illusion and material inclinations. Chanting is the process of repeating a mantra.

Maya: Fear-driven illusions or false beliefs that obscure spiritual reality.

Mindfulness: A technique in which a person becomes intentionally aware of their thoughts and actions in the present moment. A practice considered essential for developing insight and wisdom.

Moksha: In Indian religions (Hinduism, Jainism, Buddhism and Sikhism), refers to liberation from the cycle Samsara of death and rebirth and all of the suffering and limitation of worldly existence. In Hindu philosophy, it is seen as a transcendence of phenomenal being, of any sense of consciousness of time and space and causation.

Monk: One who practices asceticism; the conditioning of mind and body in cultivation of a spirit-filled life.

Namaste/Namaskar: Taken literally, it means "I bow to God in you," or "the Divine that resides in my heart bows to the same Divine who resides in your heart."

Om (AUM): The first emanation and sound of Creation. The primordial sound pervading all manifest existence. The most sacred of Hindu mantras, said by some to be the first name of God.

Pandit: A scholar, a teacher, particularly one skilled in Sanskrit and Hindu law, religion and philosophy. In the original usage of the word, a pundit is a Hindu, almost always a Brahmin, who has memorized substantial portion of the Vedas, along with the corresponding rhythms and melodies for chanting or singing them.

Phenomena: Observable event. Any state or process known through the senses rather than by intuition or reasoning. Common phenomena associated with kundalini are hearing sounds, see lights and colors, involuntary movements and vocal outbursts.

Parabdha Karma Phenomena: Karma that has already been caused, and is in the process of being played out, expressed in the manifested phenomena of cause and effect, in both waking and in dreaming consciousness.

Prana: A Sanskrit word meaning "breath" and refers to a vital life-sustaining force of living beings and vital energy natural processes of the universe.

Pranams: Offering obeisance to the devotees of the lord.

Pranayam: Defines the regulation of the in and out flow of this vital energy. It explains that the body, breath and the mind are intricately interwoven. When the air moves, the mind moves, and when the air is stilled, the mind also could be stilled. Hence the various techniques employed in Pranayam are to stabilize the flow of air, thus to achieve the balanced state of mind.

Prema: The quality of holy and pure love, sense of strong affection or profound oneness.

Reiki: A comprehensive spiritual practice established in early 20th century Japan by Mikao Usui, based predominantly on the transmission of energy, and since hijacked within Western culture to become almost exclusively an energy healing practice.

Rudraksha mala beads: A string of 108 beads, with a "sumeru" bead functioning as a summit bead. Rudraksha is commonly used to mean the seeds of the Rudraksha tree, for counting of sacred mantra (prayers) during a period of recitation.

Sadhana: Spiritual efforts — dedication to the aim of God realization.

Sadhu: A holy man dedicated to the search for God. A sadhu may or may not be a yogi or a sannyasin, or be connected in any way with a Guru or legitimate lineage. Sadhus usually have no fixed abode and travel unattached from place to place, often living on alms. There are countless sadhus on the roads and byways, mountains and riverbanks and in ashrams and caves in India. They have, by their very existence, a profound, stabilizing effect on the consciousness of India and the world.

Sadhvi: A female sadhu.

Samadhi: A contemplative or meditative state of consciousness in which the one who meditates and the object of meditation are united as one.

Samskaras: Impressions derived from past experiences (in this life or a previous life), which then color one's nature, responses and state of mind.

Sanskrit: Classical language of India today mostly used for religious rituals, the study of ancient scriptures and philosophical writings.

Sannyas/Sannyasi: Literal translation: "laying it all down." A Hindu renunciate — one who is dedicated to the spiritual path, and who has received formal Diksha from an authorized Guru (Spiritual Teacher).

Sat Guru: Spiritual master, dispeller of darkness and illusion. An awakened one or one who rests in pure consciousness.

Satsang: Association with truth. Being in the presence of a Sat Guru or Realized Being for the purpose of spiritual knowledge and study. The company with an assembly of persons who listen to, talk about, and assimilate the truth. This practice also takes the form of listening to or reading scriptures, reflecting on, discussing and assimilating their meaning, meditating on the source of these words, and bringing their meaning into one's daily life. Especially in the tradition of advaita-vedanta, satsang with an "enlightened" master is considered to be a prerequisite.

Self: The Absolute, Parasiva, God. That which gives life to all existence.

Self-Inquiry: A process of transcending illusion of persona as separate from Self, i.e. the Absolute. The great Indian sage Ramana Maharshi emphasized self-inquiry as his main teaching. Questioning, "Who Am I?" and negating all that is impermanent, until one's attention comes to rest in the silence of the pure Awareness of the Source/Self, within the spiritual Heart Center.

Seva: Literally translated as "string" in Sanskrit, implying that all is connected and to give service to one is to give to the whole. Selfless service — giving back — work offered to God and is performed without attachment and with the attitude that one is not the doer. Seva is a cornerstone of Karma Yoga.

Shakti: Literally meaning force, power or energy. Shakti is the Hindu God as Divine Mother, representing the active, dynamic principles of feminine power.

Shanti: Inner peace (or peace of mind).

Shiva: The formless, timeless and spaceless Supreme God, also known as "The Pure One" or "Pure Consciousness."

Siddha: A siddha is one who has attained a siddhi. The siddhis are paranormal abilities considered to be emergent abilities of an individual that is on the path to siddhahood, and do not define a siddha, who is established in the spiritual substratum of creation. The siddhi in its pure form is the attainment of flawless identity with Reality (Braham); perfection of the spirit, unity with The Absolute.

Swami: Literally means "one with the self" — used as a title of respect for a Hindu religious teacher or renunciate.

Tapas: austerity.

Vairagya: Sanskrit word for non-attachment.

Vipassana: Means "extraordinary vision." A simple but powerful meditation technique that depends on direct experience and observation of the mind and senses. The practice can develop a deep understanding of the impermanence of reality and diminish deep-seated complexes.

Viveka: mental discrimination — the power to discriminate the true (what is permanent) from the false (impermanent).

Yoga: Literally meaning union with the Divine, yoga is a family of ancient spiritual practices including karma yoga (yoga of action), Jhana yoga (yoga of knowledge), Bhakti yoga (yoga of devotion) and Raja yoga (yoga of meditation). Outside of India, yoga has become primarily associated with the practice of Hatha yoga postures, a system that developed in India to prepare students of the practice of Raja yoga.

Glossary

Swami-G and Swami Siddhananda in Rishikesh, India.

For inquiries about donations, energy work, satsang or kundalini, please write:

>Guru Swami-G (Ganga Karmokar)
>
>crystalkundalini@hotmail.com

>Swami Siddhananda
>
>pianojanie@yahoo.com

Other books by Ganga Karmokar:

Kundalini, From Hell to Heaven

Song of the Butterfly: Finding the Freedom From Within

Truth Unbound

www.ingramcontent.com/pod-product-compliance
Lightning Source LLC
Chambersburg PA
CBHW060501090426
42735CB00011B/2071